The Horse Has Six Legs

T0048839

Other Books by Charles Simic

Poetry
Sixty Poems
That Little Something
My Noiseless Entourage
The Voice at 3:00 A.M.: Selected Late & New Poems
Night Picnic
Jackstraws
Selected Early Poems
Walking the Black Cat
A Wedding in Hell
Hotel Insomnia
The Book of Gods and Devils
The World Doesn't End: Prose Poems
Unending Blues
Weather Forecast for Utopia and Vicinity
Selected Poems
Austerities
Classic Ballroom Dances
Charon's Cosmology
Return to a Place Lit by a Glass of Milk
Dismantling the Silence

Prose
The Renegade: Writings on Poetry and a Few Other Things
The Monster Loves His Labyrinth: Notebooks
Dime-Store Alchemy: The Art of Joseph Cornell
Metaphysician in the Dark
A Fly in the Soup: Memoirs
Orphan Factory: Essays and Memoirs
The Unemployed Fortune-Teller: Essays and Memoirs
The Uncertain Certainty: Interviews, Essays, and Notes on Poetry

Translations
Dark Things: Poems by Novica Tadić
A Wake for the Living: Poems by Radmila Lazić
Devil's Lunch: Selected Poems by Aleksandar Ristović
Night Mail: Selected Poems by Novica Tadić
Homage to the Lame Wolf by Vasko Popa

The Horse Has Six Legs

An Anthology of Serbian Poetry

UPDATED AND EXPANDED

Edited, Translated, and with an Introduction by
Charles Simic

Graywolf Press

Some of the new poems included in this updated and expanded edition of *The Horse Has Six Legs* first appeared in *Field,* the *New Yorker,* and *TriQuarterly.*

Publication of this volume is made possible in part by a grant provided by the Minnesota State Arts Board, through an appropriation by the Minnesota State Legislature; a grant from the Wells Fargo Foundation Minnesota; and a grant from the National Endowment for the Arts, which believes that a great nation deserves great art. Significant support has also been provided by Target; the McKnight Foundation; and other generous contributions from foundations, corporations, and individuals. To these organizations and individuals we offer our heartfelt thanks.

Published by Graywolf Press
250 Third Avenue North, Suite 600
Minneapolis, MN 55401
All rights reserved.

www.graywolfpress.org

Published in the United States of America

ISBN 978-1-55597-557-9

2 4 6 8 9 7 5 3 1
First Graywolf Printing, 2010

Library of Congress Control Number: 2010920763

Cover design: Kyle G. Hunter

Cover art: Ivana Vukanovic. Courtesy of Crazygoat Promotions.

CONTENTS

Rade Drainac

Vasko Popa

Radmila Lazić

Novica Tadić

Milan Djordjević

Introduction to the Updated and Expanded Edition

This new expanded Serbian anthology includes six new poets and a number of additional poems by poets already included in the earlier edition. Again, I sought poets whose work seemed to me of exceptional quality and whose poems were unlike any American readers were likely to encounter at home. My motive for translating has always been very simple. It begins the moment I come across a poem in another language that strikes me as so fine that the mere thought that people who care for poetry in this country are unable to read it seems to me an injustice that needs to be remedied. Of course, wanting to translate a poem is one thing; doing justice to it is something else. Every translation is more or less a utopian project. Without quite being aware of it, a translator sets out to bridge two distinct cultures and the idiosyncrasies of two languages as if this was the most normal thing to do. It is, and it isn't. Luckily for translators, native literary traditions do not develop and thrive in total isolation. Despite numerous language and cultural barriers, the news of what poets are up to in Patagonia eventually reaches the poets in Mongolia. The Serbian poets are no different. As Radmila Lazić says: "The living and dead poets are brothers. The feeling of belonging to this brotherhood, or sisterhood, is stronger than the feeling of belonging to a nation, race, religion, gender. . . ." A shocking claim, until we remember that almost every poet we ever liked was probably both a saint and a heretic.

Yugoslavia, a country in which all these newly added poets were born and grew up thinking of themselves as Yugoslavs, ceased to exist in the 1990s in a series of bloody wars. Many of its cities and villages were destroyed; thousands of innocent people were massacred, while many more than that were expelled from their homes. Serbs, who were one of the main culprits and one of the main victims, were also divided among themselves regionally, politically, and in every other possible way that a people scattered over a large geographical area—often intermixed with other ethnic groups, and thus each having their own separate history and even culture—can be. In 1999, NATO bombed Serbia for two and a half months in order to stop the ethnic cleansing of Albanians in the disputed Serbian province of Kosovo. Military and civilian targets were struck and there were significant civilian casualties. That was followed by the overthrow of the president Slobodan Milošević in October 2000 by popular uprising, the assassination of the reformist president Zoran Djindjić in March 2003, and the continuous political turmoil and economic crises that have not significantly subsided to this day. These were the worst places to live in former Yugoslavia during these years, but in Serbia too, isolated as it was and regarded as a pariah among nations, it was difficult to have a normal life. Thousands of young, educated and professional people escaped, most of them never to return. Good books continued to be published, but their writers were rarely translated and found it near-impossible to get a visa for even a short visit abroad. Everyone knew the names of Serbian war criminals, but almost no one knew the names of its writers and poets.

How much of this unhappy history is reflected in the poetry written at the time? The answer is: not much in any obvious way. None of the poets included here jumped on the nationalist bandwagon, which produced its share of patriotic poetry. Some poets kept a low profile; others like Lazić and Milan Djordjević were active in the opposition, although their political activity is not reflected in what they wrote in any obvious way. This wariness of poetry with a political message, I imagine, stems from the memory of early communist years in Yugoslavia when poets were called upon to write poems in which the struggle of revolutionary masses against the reactionary forces of the past was depicted and exalted. This forced thoroughly dishonest and nauseating poetry in the service of some cause with which everyone was familiar from school, and it made it hard for poets in the 1990s to write overtly about the horrors that were taking place around them. And yet, the passion, the irreverence, the dark vision in the poetry of these recent poets are undoubtedly reflections of the ghastly events they have lived through. Terror, violence, and injustice are never far off, as in this poem by Danica Vukićević:

Ave

It's dangerous to live
Smell the enemy
And play up to your lover

It's dangerous to sit
On the beach and listen
To the sun loafing
It's dangerous to stroll
Touch brooding tree trunks
Shake hands in the park
And swing
It's dangerous to live
Sit on the couch
And read a book
Dangerous to think and laugh
Dangerous to yearn
And take a bath
Dangerous to look at things
Dangerous to sleep
And say no in a dream
Dangerous to be good looking
And have oneself photographed
As if death didn't exist

I forgot who said, "The poet is like a mechanic in love with the engine of his car." While their neighbors are sitting in front of the TV watching their favorite programs, the poet is in the garage or down in the street with his or her head under the hood of a parked car, changing the spark plugs, adding distilled water to the battery, adjusting the valves, and checking the ignition timing. It's an unusual vehicle whose engine runs on language, both the language of the mechanic's ancestors and the language they use today—an engine, therefore, in need of constant tuning to run properly. As for tradition, that's the junkyard where poets go to look for spare parts. I hope you understand me. As Clive James said of the great American comedian W. C. Fields, he is "one of those people who are born exiles even if they never leave home." What I find marvelous about these poets is that they are such distinct individuals. Their poems are complex, unorthodox, and unique creations compounded of their own sensibility and of elements of their own native literary tradition. As you'll discover reading this anthology, once their engines are up and running, they will take you to places that will seem both strange and familiar, the way good poems always do, and that you as a reader are not likely to forget.

Charles Simic
NEW HAMPSHIRE, 2010

Introduction to the Original Edition

Let me say at the beginning that this is not, properly speaking, a true anthology of Serbian poetry. Many important poets, both past and present, do not appear in it. The book is, rather, a selection from my thirty years of translating that poetry, and I translated only what I liked and kept only what I felt I did justice to. Representing the entire range of Serbian poetry was beyond my ambition and my ability.

Serbians—who live in the eastern part of what was known until recently as Yugoslavia—have a literature that dates back to the twelfth century. The development of their literature was interrupted by the conquest of that part of the Balkans by the Turks in the late fourteenth century. Serbians spent five hundred years under Turkish occupation. Aside from a few written poems, it was oral poetry, both the heroic ballads and the so-called women's songs (a few of which are included in this book), that flourished. They were collected and written down by Vuk Stefanović Karadžić (1787–1864), and it is these extensive collections that have served as the foundation of literary culture in Serbia. Although known to Goethe, Sir Walter Scott, Prosper Mérimée, and Pushkin in their day, only a small number of these poems has been translated. This is unfortunate, because they represent an impressive body of literature containing many individual masterpieces.

In the nineteenth century, after Serbia's liberation from the Turks, Serbian literature and poetry were influenced by romanticism and later realism and symbolism. This period produced a number of fine poets, including two extraordinary ones. Petar II Petrović Njegoš (1813–1851) is the author of the Miltonic epic *The Ray of Microcosm* and a long dramatic poem written in the decasyllable of oral poetry, *The Mountain Wreath*. The greatest poem of the century may be the magnificent "Santa Maria Della Salute" by Laza Kostić (1841–1910).

It was during the twentieth century, however, that Serbian poetry reached its fullness and distinctness. Beginning with the Parnassian Jovan Dučić (1874–1943), who after a life as a diplomat died in exile in Gary, Indiana, and the symbolist Milan Rakić (1876–1938), a number of excellent poets followed. Among them were Miloš Crnjanski (1893–1977), who was also a fine novelist, and the first truly modern poet, Rastko Petrović (1898–1949), who also died in the United States.

No period was as rich in Serbian poetry as that following the Second World War. In addition to the poets included here, I must mention Oskar Davičo (1909–1990), Stevan Raičković (1928–2007), Borislav Radović (1935–), and Milovan Danojlić (1937–). An equally interesting anthology could be made of the many excellent poets who were born after the war. I'm not exaggerating when I say that I could have easily included another dozen younger poets whose work deserves recognition abroad.

I was born in Beograd in 1938 and left when I was fifteen, returning only twice for brief visits. In my childhood I knew Serbian oral poetry, both the heroic ballads and the short lyric poems, as well as the few old standards we studied in school, but I had no knowledge whatsoever of modern poetry. My interest in Serbian poetry developed gradually in the 1960s, some years after I wrote and published my first poems in English. The 1960s were a time of great translation activity in this country, and since I knew the language, I paid a visit one day to the New York Public Library on Forty-second Street to read the Yugoslav poets. That's where I discovered their poetry and made my first translations of Popa, Lalić, and Nastasijević. I wanted to share the poems with my American friends, but I was also fascinated by the process of translation. I had already begun to wonder what kind of poems I would have written had I started writing poetry in Serbian. Are the differences between the two languages on the surface, or is it true what they say about language, that each one paints the world in a different way?

Translation is an actor's medium. If I cannot make myself believe that I'm writing the poem that I'm translating, no degree of aesthetic admiration for the work can help me. Imaginative affinity is what one needs to accomplish that identification and risk the impossible. In a successful translation, one indeed does, at times, become the Other.

There's the additional problem of translating from a small language and an unfamiliar culture into a larger one. The essence of a culture is not entirely embodied in language. There's the complicated associative context that makes the translation of a French lyric poem easier than that of a medieval Serbian one.

My first rule has always been to be as literal as possible. When it is not idiomatic, one seeks an equivalent to convey the spirit of the original. Little said, much meant, is what poetry is all about. An idiom is the lair of the tribal beast. It carries its familiar smells. We are here in the realm of submerged and elusive meanings that do not correspond to any actual word on the page. Lyricism, in its true sense, is the awe before the untranslatable. Like childhood, it is a language that cannot be replaced by another language. A great lyric poem approaches untranslatability.

Did these translations influence my poetry? Of course they did. Reading these poems closely, as only a translator in love with the original can read them, I was experiencing their way of looking at the world and making art. There's no question that I recognized a part of myself in the poems. A complicated psychic translation was taking place each time I undertook to translate. I was returning to my psychic roots with English words in my mouth. I realized how much I was still a part of that universe, how much I no longer was. It occurred to me that in pursuit of self-knowledge I should be spending my entire life translating a few Serbian poems.

They say that each translator is like the one who wants to disseminate the Gospels. I, too, bring glad tidings. There are still poets and beautiful poems to be discovered and read with lasting pleasure in this vile old world.

Charles Simic
NEW HAMPSHIRE, 1992

The Horse Has Six Legs

Nobody reads poetry anymore,
so who the hell are you
I see bent over this book?
—ALEKSANDAR RISTOVIĆ

I FOUND THIS POEM many years ago, as I recall, in a book of medieval Serbian literature. I have never been able to find it again, nor has anyone else, as far as I know. Jerome Rothenberg published it in 1970 in *Alcheringa* as a translation, so it must be one.

The Message of King Sakis and the Legend
of the Twelve Dreams He Had in One Night

1

I saw a gold pillar from earth to heaven.

2

I saw a dark towel
hanging from heaven to earth.

3

I saw three boiling kettles:
one of oil, one of butter, and one of water,
and oil boiled over into butter,
and butter into water
but the water boiled all by itself.

4

I saw an old mare with her colt,
and a black eagle pulling grass by its roots
and laying it down before the mare
while the colt neighed.

5

I saw a bitch lying on a dunghill
while the puppies barked from her womb.

6

I saw many monks soaked in pitch
wailing because they can't get out.

7
I saw a beautiful horse
grazing with two heads
one in front, one in the back.

8
I saw precious stones, pearls and royal wreaths
scattered over the whole kingdom,
but fire came down from heaven
and scorched everything into ashes.

9
I saw the rich giving workers either
gold or silver or rice,
but when they asked for their own reward,
no one was left.

10
I saw evil-faced rocks descending
from the sky
and walking all over the earth.

11
I saw three maidens in a mowed field
bearing wreaths of sunlight on their heads
and sweet-smelling flowers in their hands.

12
I saw men with slits for eyes,
cruel fingernails, and hair that rose up,
and these were the devil's servants.

ORAL POETRY, WOMEN'S SONGS

These folk poems are of uncertain date. They were collected in the late eighteenth and early nineteenth centuries, but undoubtedly originated much earlier.

Brotherless Sisters

Two sisters who had no brother
Made one of silk to share,
Of white silk and of red.
For his waist they used barberry wood.
Black eyes, two precious stones.
For eyebrows sea leeches.
Tiny teeth a string of pearls.
They fed him sugar and honey sweet
And told him: now eat and then speak.

The smallest basil leaf was heard to whimper:
Silent dew, won't you fall on me?
I fell on you two days in a row,
But today I was distracted watching
The mountain fairy quarrel with an eagle.
The fairy said, the mountain is mine.
The eagle said, no, it is mine.
The fairy broke the eagle's wings.
The eaglets in the nest cried bitterly,
Bitterly they cried in their sorrow.
Don't cry, eaglets in the nest, I said,
I'll take you to the land of India
Where amaranth grows to the horses' knees,
Sweet clover to their shoulders
And the sun never sets.
At that the eaglets were consoled.

The sky is strewn with stars
And the wide meadow with sheep.
The sheep have no shepherd
Except for crazy Radoye
And he has fallen asleep.
His sister Janja wakes him:
Get up, crazy Radoye,
Your sheep have wandered off.
Let them, sister, let them.
The witches have feasted on me,
Mother carved my heart out,
Our aunt held the torch for her.

A girl threw an apple to a cloud,
And the cloud kept the apple.
The girl prayed to all the clouds:
Brother clouds, give me back my golden apple.
The guests have arrived:
My mother's brothers and my uncles.
Their horses are wild like mountain fairies.
When they tread the dust
The dust doesn't rise.
When they tread on water,
Their hooves don't get wet.

There smoke, sooty smoke,
There is your door,
And fried egg,
And bread and butter,
And your grandpa's bones
With which to prick yourself.

Plow, Maro, the plains,
And sow your sorrows.
If marigold grows for you
Wither darling for me.
If sweet basil grows for you
Come to me on bare feet tonight.
If violets grow for you,
We'll kiss until tomorrow.

Wind blows, one can smell the wild rosemary.
It seems to me my love is coming.
If I knew from what direction
I'd sow sweet basil in his path,
Red roses where there is no path.
Let my love come by their scent,
By their scent and not by the light of day.

MOMČILO NASTASIJEVIĆ

[1894–1938]

At the age of ten Nastasijević started playing the flute and later took up the violin. A volunteer in the Serbian army in the First World War, he studied Serbian linguistics in Belgrade and in Paris. Nastasijević wrote little poetry, but all of his work is of unmistakable originality and perfection. He worked as a professor of high-school French and also wrote short stories and essays on poetry.

To My Dead Sister

Saturday, the sorrow's killing me,
attend to me, mother.

Roses that she embroidered
to ease her suffering,
like blood spots on the wall
in the lamp's shadow.
Attend to me, mother.

In the corner where the nurse sang,
an air of hope, a strand of it,
her string, didn't you hear, broken?
Attend to me, mother.

Not where shadows are in penitence,
but here among us you seek rest
where, innocent, you hurt, sister,
where, all pale, you passed away.

Or did the pain martyr you?
A drop of kind oil in healing from the unknown
for our candle to burn,
here where your pain still abides, sister,
where, all pale, you passed away.

Saturday, sorrow's killing me,
attend to me, mother.

Still Trees

All hurts. Dear friends,
is it for me you keep still?
Not a leaf to wound me with its shiver.

Quietly, even more quietly,
the wound's healing
seals me into speech.

I embrace the trees in turn
like brothers.
I stroke their scars.

Dear friends,
does it hurt when the ax
cuts into your bark?

Does it heal
when for your mute
I cry out in anguish?

If this is blasphemy,
forgive me.
A heart was given to me.

Is it for me you keep still?
Quietly, even more quietly
with the wound's healing,
in anguish, friends,
for all of you mute

to high heavens
in a whisper I pass
the good tidings.

Gray Moment

And suddenly, all turns gray
as if burnt through,
and yet all lives on.

Secret friend, listen,
this silently aching heart
pushes away past all that dread.

And you, who after me
and in ignorance,
tread this strange path:

It is gray there,
grayness cuts to the quick,
gray are the eyes of the secret.

And when the trees begin to die,
there's neither grief nor warning,
just a dry leaf
which strangely with its hush

soothes the sufferer's forehead.

Roadside Fountain

Trickling, trickling
drop by tiny drop in welcome.

At dawn when to my call, sister,
it winds away,
in sorrow to answer at dusk,
turned crimson.

Trickling, trickling
drop by tiny drop in welcome.

When as a bridegroom I lead
the drunken wedding guests,
blood squirts into tassels,
unveiled, O sister,
the bride is drying in my arms.

All pale we bury her at night,
my heart numb
for some wail still to come.

Trickling, trickling
drop by tiny drop in welcome.

It draws near; I'll get over it.
Not a thread of myself
for the earth to squander.

You'll know me, sister, when in the evening
without a bride or wedding guest,
my steps trickle by crimson.

Burial

1
The bugle's for him:
laid out in a coffin—
his face yellow.

His army buddies—
rough cloth against their skin,
fingers drumming.

And the sky is blue—
and the shadows
make the road pretty.

2
They buried him properly.
Stuck a wooden cross,
then a name: Subotić Stano,
legibly written

so his mother or wife
can find him,
and whoever else loves him.

3
The bugle's for him:
laid out in a coffin—
his face yellow.

And the sky is blue—
and the shadows
make the road pretty.

from **Deaf Things**

1
Not one whisper
not one cry,
out of this dread

when to the sky above
or the hell below
the heart strives mute.

O be still,
my much-too-heavy—
make me even more stonelike
dull-echoing stone.

2
It has hardened,
it trembles at times strangely,
it'll boil over

even by drop only,
by a drop
the unsayable into a word,

at once
to drown each creature,
each thing.

O be still, still.
Not one whisper,
not one cry.

3
I know by the arrow of darkness
the day broke
inside a stone.

Struck dumb,
with a breath of unknown
the day cleared.

6
Beauty since
it blinds,
leaves dumb.

Deeper thus,
hurting with you,
with my life's
dull-echoing dread,
I'd speak.

Extinction itself—
I'd dare
descend into its root.

Late into the night,
into the day, I'd keep
watch over you,
dumb and heavy with you.

In my foot's fall
my steps hushes with you.
It's a mute road I travel.

10
Pain
so it turned black.

I want, since it happens,
for this wound,
to be living to its depths.

Out of this hell
for a breath of some paradise—
out of this sin
for someone to become a saint.

For this suffering
and muddle
to have no end.

For the sake of that grace,
forever, this curse.

The String

1
Something muffled,
barely audible
within me happens.

Broken, silenced,
in death
the string gives voice.

2
With honey or bile,
the glass is full,
it hurts me:

I drink it up,
and die with the ineffable
into words.

3
Not only I,
but a brother
in ignorance,
whom, even more tacitly,
this secrecy
makes suffer.

4
I know
where the heart beats
of gold or bronze
slowly the Son is crucified.

Singing or weeping
secretly
his crown is woven.

5
Something muffled,
barely audible
within me happens.

Broken, silenced
in death
the string gives voice.

ALEKSANDAR VUČO

[1897–1985]

Vučo studied in Paris and was a member of the Serbian sur-
realist group. In the 1930s he edited a Marxist-Surrealist
journal. *Cyril and Methodius* was published in 1932. He
wrote many books of poems and was also a fine novelist.

from **Cyril and Methodius**

Cyril and Methodius
Two parade-like piously eye-bulging saints
Under bloody halos of nails-thorns
On long and hairy legs of clear night
Partly soloists partly twin-choirs
Climb the godless mountain

Crustacean twigs yelp down the barren Golgotha of the holy steps
Painfully wail the veins—whores in permanent adultery with a pack of
    aroused animals
In the bed of trees and by the edge of blind Christian frog ponds
Ripen the deep kisses of dawn
Whose humble heart—Our Father in Heaven—would rustle with the
    leaves of this forest
So that the poor shy colt doesn't spit disgusted into its own eye
And grab the lustful second wife of some Moslem
Before the rapacious mocking scissors of madness
In the deep box-shrub-lined paths and mountain passes
Where tonight sin swarms—

Cyril and Methodius
In the Edenlike globe of mustered heuristic thoughts
Parade-like with eyes piously bulging
Stoically push through the sinful meeting place in the forest
So that through stubborn temptation and frequent appearance of chronic lust
They may reach that distant goal

DESANKA MAKSIMOVIĆ

[1898–1993]

Since her first book in 1924, Maksimović was at one time
the most popular and widely read poet in the country. She
studied in Paris, taught at a women's high school, and pub-
lished more than twenty collections of poetry. She also
wrote novels and essays.

Snake

Under the dry swath
a snake crawled out.
Around her the empty meadow
and one flower.
Above, two, three clouds,
a bird flying,
the sun shining.

On the road winding into the distance,
someone's song.
The lonely sound entangles itself
in the grass.
She listens, her head raised
wide-awake into the air.
The sun is shining.

Here's where they killed her mother
with the blade of a scythe.
They'll do the same to her
when she crawls out of the shrubbery.
Her clothes will rot
with their embroideries
and the glow of dew.

Even in eternity, never again
will the same snake sun itself,
nor will the same birds fly,
nor the same flower sprout.
The sun is shining.

Darkness

Darkness was born in the forest. I found it there
when from the shady ravine I crawled on all fours.
I trembled together with the white flower by the pond.
The last light sadly flowed
through the tops of the fir trees.

In fear no one noticed, even though it stood at the edge of the forest,
That the dark is the silent midnight ghost,
the primeval forest's spider knight,
the hungry dragon.

Somewhere countless tiny plants and creatures drown,
and the trees draw together in close and gloomy councils.
All in vain. The darkness pushed through the pines
and like an evil spirit started for the village
down the dusty roads.

The top of fir trees grow numb like giant candles.
Only the water flower still shines pale like a drowned star.
One could hear then the terrifying forest birds
announcing the night, the way the roosters announce the day.

Bloody Fable

It happened in some peasant land
In the hilly Balkans,
A troupe of schoolboys
Died a martyr's death in a single day.

All were born in the same year.
And their school days were identical:
Together they were taken
To the same celebrations,
Together they were inoculated
Against the same illness,
And they all died in the same way.

It happened in some peasant land
In the hilly Balkans,
A troupe of schoolboys
Died a martyr's death in a single day.

Fifty minutes before the moment of their death,
They still sat in their seats,
That troupe of schoolboys,
Solving the same difficult problem:
How far can a traveler traveling on foot . . .
And so forth.

Their heads were full of the same numbers,
And their bags full of notebooks
With good and bad grades.
The same dreams, the same secrets
Patriotic and romantic
Lay pressed in their pockets.
To all of them, it seemed, that long, long

They'll run under the blue sky
Until all the quizzes in the world are solved.

It happened in some peasant land
In the hilly Balkans
A troupe of schoolboys
Died a martyr's death in a single day.
Whole rows of boys took each other by the hand,
And from the last class
Calmly walked before the firing squad
As if death were nothing.
Whole rows of friends rose at the same time
To their eternal abode.

For Maria Magdalenes

Tzar Dušan,
I ask pardon
for women who were stoned,
for their accomplices
dark nights, smell of clover,
leaves where they fell
intoxicated
like quail or woodcock,
I ask for their scorned lives
for the pity not given them
and their heartache.

I ask pardon
for moonlight and rubies
of their skin,
and their dusks,
sudden showers, unbraided hair,
for their arms like silver branches
for their loves
undressed and damned—
for all Maria Magdalenes.

RADE DRAINAC

[1899–1943]

Drainac was a famous Belgrade bohemian who spent his life in the taverns of the city, often playing the violin. He served in the Serbian army in the First World War. His first book, *Purple Laughter,* was published in 1920. He wrote three more collections of poetry, plus a novel and a war diary. He was influenced by Apollinaire, Cendrars, and Esenin. He died of consumption.

My hunger is infinite and my hands always empty.

Down city streets I carry at night the moon on my fingers
and leave my sadness under the windows of unhappy women.

I would give everything and yet I have nothing.
My hunger is infinite and my hands always empty.

from **Opus III**

Dreams worn out like small coins taken out of circulation.
Like unfaithful women they betrayed humanity.
Not even beggars can warm their hands any longer on their fires.
Unreasonable ideals led us into the abyss.
At times the thought was only a road sign.

Thought!
To the flunky it appears heavier than a wheel of a truck.
It would drag it the way children drag toys.
That metal, however, is lighter than the thinnest insurance policy.
The moths in the library are proud of it,
And the wrinkled old men behind whose pince-nez
The cold earth stretches from here to Siberia.

I want to tell you about body parts.
There's true celestial mechanics in the gaps between them.
The heart resembles a washed handkerchief,
White only because it dries beneath the clouds of thought.

It wakes us at night like a nightingale
And when it has no feathers, it resembles a rooster
from whose beak dark blood drips.
Heart!
Even to the ant it seems heavier than Halley's Comet.
The caterpillar imagines it as a Legion of Honor.
The heart of a woman under the true weight of her breast full of milk!
The heart of a young girl!
If it fools you, you win through tears
which dissolve every suffering by their salt.

There are intestines like tangled road
On which tramps sing.
Arias of the empty stomach behind the street corner
Like the barking of village dogs:
They tie the people of all races into one Being.
All that endless chewing is the only philosophy.
Chewing and burping!
There's no room anymore for frivolous thought
And senseless dreaming.

One day, when philosophy kicks the bucket,
We'll lie on the clouds like cows on the meadows.
Our thoughts we'll return from the daily Crusades
And dreams will fall asleep on our bodies
Like badgers in a cornfield.

But today . . . see how the crowlike clouds hover over the city!
I don't wish to know about cute phantoms as long as cannons are taken
    for crooners,
As long as soldier's jackets are sewn so wearily,
As long as the dampness of city buildings won't save us,
Grim dungeons in which to eat bread!
Don't call me a loving brother
Since my youth I slept on the bed of hate.
I search for a man, and not for god.
And my flag is Revenge.

The victory of rich harvest and the gold of our fields.
All my yearning is in the evenings when it rains heavily.
Like the idlest man in the world who counts his heartbeats,
I sing often of heaven's blue curtains
over our Balkan forests.

It seems to me that life is only a commentary on this poem,
A lost shadow among the trees in the woods.
That's why I whistle like a hoodlum down the streets at night
Since I don't have any prejudices,
Superstitions.
I keep only to the line of life in my hand.
Left! Right!
No my dear. I stick labels only to suitcases.

Landscape

The rooster crowed with his beak stuck in the sky
when the locomotive sped down the plains
for the last time the night watchman and the moon
strolled down the small town street
the dawn smelled of warm bread
at the factory gates the day was being born
the day that found the beggar on the bridge
and his dream torn like a cloud in autumn

with one final effort the woman in the hospital
gave birth to the sun—
the white smile of the newborn—
all the doors in the city opened at that instant

Leaf

I've changed stations: autumn remained behind and my bags.
The sky now is doubtful like an awkward lie.
In the first tavern I'll need to forget
the melancholy letter that woke me from my sleep.
Idle, I stagger down the street past offices.
The swallows have flown and the typewriters have stayed.
One the horizon there is a huge trumpet of smoke.
A plane has just been invented as small as a butterfly.
Bravo! That's a good sign.
The first autumn leaf falls on my hat.

from **When the Poet without Lying Verses in His Heart Returns to His Native Country**

. . . Then the drops were freezing on black branches of ancient ash trees
The dog barked at the moon and the stars were cold in the snow flowers
    on the windowpane
We all had worries and sinful dreams
About life and our cursed blood . . .

In the spring with the first clod of earth
The days carried us off through the ice in all directions
With a song in the woods or with the bull in the mill.
I was never a good son, drunk I stepped out of a tavern
To kiss someone's heavy breasts in the churchyard under the moon
Today I wish a vulture would peck my heart spiked on a dry branch
On the horizon where the polar star sings over the river,
Over the river and the blue juniper bush.

. . . Once I loved the dew, wet grass and the quince tree.
(The time has passed when both of us sang wildly working in the vineyard.)
Her husband is a barrel maker (they say he loves his wife).
In her yard there are children, in my life wild ferns.
I converse with birds.
To no one do I dare confide what I do . . .

If I were a horse thief or the switchman at the village station,
The ferryman on the river or the stone carver in the church of St. Petka,
The quince would be mine, I would have willpower
To sing when the leaves are falling
From the bird cage they call life.

This way . . . I count over my dreams, listen to crows and owls,
And listen to dogs bark at me . . .

. . . Then, I was young: my heart was red as the blossom of a sour cherry.
Now the earth cracks and the apple trees' broken branches . . .
Behind the fence there is a sunflower.
Crows sleep on it.
On the dead hearth I burnt the dry branch of a plum tree.
Over the fields rain falls; by the village, a cemetery and a road:
My heart
Where will we go now . . .

In a forest in which the bull is the only violin . . .

Classic Verses

I would need a distance of a hundred years
To learn all the horrors I was contemporary to.
What is the surrender of Mycenae with its lemon tree blossoms,
The fall of Troy and destruction of Pergamum
Behind which the bloody Greek hid himself?
Don't curse me if you see me alone
Walking away from the rest of you people
Down the road by which hawthorn flower.
And do no be surprised
If you see me gazing at the starry sky
While standing on our black earth.

It'd be better, better, if I had not been born
Before the evil winds of human blood ceased!
That way I'd be the first happy man
Who hid himself from his fate
In the fiery will of gods who show themselves only
When they want to reveal their miracle infinity.
Who of us knows why we are born and why we wander
In the huge pain of the world, mute like Buddha.

VASKO POPA

[1922–1991]

The most widely translated and best-known postwar Yugoslav poet. He was born in Grebenac near the Rumanian border and died in Belgrade. Popa was educated in Bucharest, Vienna, and Belgrade. During the Second World War he was imprisoned by the Nazis. Influenced by French surrealism, his best-known books are *Crust* (1953), *Restless Field* (1954), and *Wolf Salt* (1975). He was the editor of three influential anthologies of folk material, Serbian humor, and poets' dreams.

from the cycle **Games**

Hide-and-Seek

Someone hides from someone else
Hides under his own tongue
The other looks for him under the earth

He hides himself on his forehead
The other looks for him in the sky

He hides in his forgetfulness
The other looks for him in the grass

Looks for him looks
There's no place he doesn't look
And looking loses himself

Rose Thieves

Someone is a rose bush
The others are wind's daughters
The others are rose thieves

The rose thieves sneak up to the rose
One of them steals it
Hides it in his heart

The wind's daughters appear
See the picked beauty
And run after the thieves

They open their hearts one by one
In one they find a heart
In another so-help-me nothing

They open and open their chests
Until they find a heart
And in that heart a stolen rose

Hunter

Someone enters without knocking
Enters into someone's ear
And comes out through the other

Comes with the step of a matchstick
With the step of a lit matchstick
And circles the head inside

He's the boss

Someone enters without knocking
Enters into someone's ear
And doesn't come out through the other

He's caught

Ashes

Some are nights the others ashes

Each night sets fire to its own star
And dances a black dance around it
Until the star burns out

Then the nights divide themselves
Some become stars
Others remain nights

Again each night sets fire to its own star
And dances a black dance around it
Until the star burns out

The last night becomes both star and night
It sets fire to itself
And dances the black dance around itself

from the cycle **Yawn of Yawns**

Forgetful Number

Once upon a time there was a number
Pure and round like the sun
But lonely very lonely

It started to calculate by itself

It divided it multiplied
Subtracted and added itself
But remained always alone

It stopped calculating
And shut itself away
In its rounded sunlit innocence

The flowing tracks of its calculations
Stayed outside

They began to hunt each other in the dark
To divide themselves while multiplying
To subtract themselves while adding

That's the way it goes in the dark

No one was left to plead to it
To call back its tracks
And rub them out

Proud Error

Once upon a time there was an error
So ridiculous so minute
No one could have paid attention to it

It couldn't stand
To see or hear itself

It made up all sorts of nonsense
Just to prove
That it really didn't exist

It imagined a space
To fit all its proofs in
And time to guard its proofs
And the world to witness them

All that it imagined
Was not so ridiculous
Or so minute
But was of course in error

Was anything else possible

The Tale about a Tale

Once upon a time there was a tale

It came to the end
Before its beginning
And began
After its end

Its heroes entered it
After their death
And left it
Before their birth

Its heroes spoke
Of an earth of a heaven
They spoke a lot

Only they didn't say
What even they didn't know
That they were heroes in a tale

In a tale coming to the end
Before its beginning
And beginning
After its end

Burning Shewolf

1

On the bottom of the sky
The shewolf lies

Body of living sparks
Overgrown with grass
And covered with sun's dust

In her breasts
Mountains rise threatening
And forgive as they lower themselves

Through her veins rivers thunder
In her eyes lakes flash

In her boundless heart
The ores melt with love
On seven stems of their fire

Before the first and last howl
Wolves play on her back
And live in her crystal womb

2

They cage the shewolf
In the earth's fire

Force her to build
Towers of smoke
Make bread out of coals

They fatten her with embers
And have her wash it down
With hot milk of mercury

They force her to mate
With red-hot pokers
And rusty old drills

With her teeth the shewolf reaches
The blonde braid of a star
And climbs back to the base of the sky

3
They catch the shewolf in steel traps
Sprung from horizon to horizon

Tear out her golden muzzle
And pluck the secret grasses
Between her thighs

They sic on her all-tied-up
Deadbeats and bloodhounds
To go ahead and rape her

Cut her up into pieces
And abandon her
To the carcass-eating tongs

With her severed tongue the shewolf
Scoops live water from the jaws of a cloud
And again becomes whole

4

The shewolf bathes herself in the blue
And washes away the ashes of dogs

On the bottom of a torrent
That runs down the stones of her motionless face
Lightnings spawn

In her wide-open jaw
The moon hides its ax during the day
The sun its knives at night

The beatings of her copper-heart
Quiet the barking distances
And lull to sleep the chirping air

In the ravines
Below her wooded eyebrows
The thunder gets ready

5

The shewolf stands on her back legs
At the base of the sky

She stands up together with wolves
Turned to stone in her womb

She stands up slowly
Between noon and midnight
Between two wolf lairs

Stands up with pain
Freeing her snout from one lair
And from the other her huge tail

She stands up with a salt-choked howl
From her dry throat

Stands up dying of thirst
Toward the clear point at the summit of the sky
The watering place of the long-tailed stars

The Little Box

The little box gets her first teeth
And her little length
Little width little emptiness
And all the rest she has

The little box continues growing
The cupboard that she was inside
Is now inside her

And she grows bigger bigger bigger
Now the room is inside her
And the house and the city and the earth
And the world she was in before

The little box remembers her childhood
And by a great great longing
She becomes a little box again

Now in the little box
You have the whole world in miniature
You can easily put in a pocket
Easily steal it easily lose it

Take care of the little box

The Admirers of the Little Box

Sing little box

Don't let sleep overtake you
The world's awake within you

In your four-sided emptiness
We turn distance into nearness
Forgetfulness into memory

Don't let your nails come loose

For the very first time
Through your keyhole
We watch sights beyond this world

Turn your key in our mouths
Swallow words and numbers
Out of your song

Don't let your lid fly open
Your bottom drop

Sing little box

The Craftsmen of the Little Box

Don't open the little box
Heaven's hat will fall out of her

Don't close her for any reason
She'll bite the trouser-leg of eternity

Don't drop her on the earth
The sun's eggs will break inside her

Don't throw her in the air
Earth's bones will break inside her

Don't hold her in your hands
The dough of the stars will go sour inside her

What are you doing for God's sake
Don't let her get out of your sight

The Owners of the Little Box

Line the inside of the little box
With your precious skin
And make yourself cozy
Just as you would in your own home

Make space voyages inside her
Gather stars make time squirt its milk
And sleep in the clouds

Just don't go around pretending
You're more important than her length
And wiser than her width

If you do we'll sell for a song
Your box and everything inside her
to the first skinner the wind

We don't care about profit
And we don't keep spoiled goods

So don't keep saying
It's we who told you this
From inside the little box

The Tenants of the Little Box

Throw into the little box
A stone
You'll take out a bird

Throw in your shadow
You'll take out the shirt of happiness

Throw in your father's root
You'll take out the axle of the universe

The little box works for you

Throw into the little box
A mouse
You'll take out a quaking hill

Throw in your mother pearl
You'll take out the chalice of eternal life

Throw in your head
You'll take out two

The little box works for you

The Enemies of the Little Box

Don't bow down to the little box
That supposedly contains everything
Your star and all other stars

Empty yourself
In her emptiness

Take two nails out of her
And give them to the owners
To eat

Make a hole in her middle
And stick on your clapper

Fill her with blueprints
And the skin of her craftsmen
And trample on her with both feet

Tie her to a cat's tail
And chase the cat

Don't bow down to the little box
If you do
You'll never straighten yourself out again

The Victims of the Little Box

Not even in a dream
Should you have anything to do
With the little box

If you saw her full of stars once
You'd wake up
Without heart or soul in your chest

If you slid your tongue
Into her keyhole once
You'd wake up with a hole in your forehead

If you ground her to bits once
Between your teeth
You'd get up with a square head

If you ever saw her empty
You'd wake up
With a belly full of mice and nails

If in a dream you had anything to do
With the little box
You'd be better off never waking up again

The Judges of the Little Box

to Karl Max Osotjić

Why do you stare at the little box
That in her emptiness
Holds the whole world

If the little box holds
The world in her emptiness
Then the antiworld
Holds the little box in its antihand

Who'll bite off the antiworld's antihand
And on that hand
Five hundred antifingers

Do you believe
You'll bite it off
With your thirty-two teeth

Or are you waiting
For the little box
To fly into your mouth

Is this why you are staring

The Benefactors of the Little Box

We'll return the little box
Into the arms
Of her inconspicuously honest properties

We won't do anything
Against her will
We'll simply take her apart

We'll crucify her
On her own cross

Pierce her bloated emptiness
And let her ooze
All the blue cosmic blood she gathered

We'll sweep her clean of stars
And antistars
And everything else that rots inside her

We won't make her suffer
We'll simply put her together again

We'll give back to the little box
Her pure inconspicuousness

The Prisoners of the Little Box

Open little box

We kiss your bottom and cover
Keyhole and key

The whole world lies crumpled in you
It resembles everything
Except itself

Not even your clear-sky mother
Would recognize it anymore

The rust will ear your key
Our world and us there inside
And finally you too

We kiss your four sides
And four corners
And twenty-four nails
And anything else you have

Open little box

Last News about the Little Box

The little box that contains the world
Fell in love with herself
And conceived
Still another little box

The little box of the little box
Also fell in love with herself
And conceived
Still another little box

And so it went on forever

The world from the little box
Ought to be inside
The last offspring of the little box

But not one of the little boxes
Inside the little box in love with herself
Is the last one

Let's see you find the world now

MIODRAG PAVLOVIĆ

[1928–]

A prolific poet, essayist, editor, stage director, and playwright. Pavlović studied medicine and his first book, *87 Poems,* was published in 1952. His most famous books of poems are *Great Scythia* (1969) and *New Scythia* (1970). Much translated, he has two books in English from New Rivers Press: *The Conqueror of Constantinople* (1976) and *The Slavs beneath Parnassus* (1985).

Questionnaire of Sleeplessness

Who rattles in the keyhole?
Who builds belfries under my window?
Who weeps over the evil fate of the hero?
Who lets lambs out of the gate?
Who drives the dwarfs out to pasture?
Who threw the King's dolls into the coffin?
Who gave the alarm clock to the bat?
Answer!
Small night celebrates the great night.
Winter. At the inn everyone is hurrying.
The messenger in armor stumbled and fell.
Who will show me tomorrow the way?
Who will cook my lunch and hand me a letter?
Who rings now above my bed
and calls for the doctor?
Or does he summon the pilgrims to witness?
Who lights the big fence of kindlings?
The dawn already wiggles under my pillow.
Who has sent the urgent invitation to suffer?
And why has that invitation been directed to me?

Morning Inscription

The day breaks.

I won't tell you who I am.
(In a whisper: a scribe.)
I go for water.

I've spent the long night reading
by candlelight.

I lower the bucket into the purple river.
Above, the sentry watches
in case the fairies try to cross.
The wind stands at city gates
with a scroll of today's news.

I see through the open window,
the master sleeps with his hand on his sword.

His body, too, is a sword.
I say it and raise my eyes.

The bedding in which god slept
whitens above.

A hand descends on my head.
Day breaks.
I have to make my bed.
Great is my joy.

MILORAD PAVIĆ

[1929–2009]

Pavić is better known as a novelist than as a poet. His novel *Dictionary of the Khazars* was translated into every European language and has been an international best seller. He published another novel and several collections of stories as well as a history of Serbian baroque literature. His first book of poems is *Palimpsests* (1967); the poems in this group are taken from his second, *The Moon Stone*.

Great Serbian Migration 1690

On Sunday we buried the icons
   except for one tasting of milk
   that weeps with eyes of its breasts
   and feeds with its starry tear

On Sunday we walled our books into the tower
   except for one that can be read in the mirror of holy water
On Sunday we tied the birds into bells to ring after us
   but the bell of our Despot we took along

   since his word it utters when upside down it tolls
On Sunday we scattered the monks over the province
   except for the one who understood the holy bell
We took him on our ship to divine the message of our Despot
   and at black cock's crowing we prayed for southern wind
   and received what we prayed for and at white cock's crow
   we regretted what we asked for

For each bird that flies over the river
   is the bridge for our thoughts
   and every butterfly a letter to our eyes,
While here we dwell deprived of our homeland

   and find no bridge back to ourselves
Wild apples tumble as though horses pass in a gallop
   through a garden
   while birds' feathers burn in flight and throughout the night
   but we don't care
whether we will understand the words of holy books
   frozen above the river

when they thaw and thunder again
and the name of holy Despot is pronounced again
by the bell
Like a shield we raise the icon with salt-eyes pure with tears

On her we see only the earth's black winds
black bulls in the offing, where they graze the foam
off the waves
where they graze flying-fish.

from **Holy Mass for Relja Krilatica**

First Song

Rejoice you who sleep with a finger in your ear
Good tidings will come to you
For you are the one who tied a knot in his own moustache
So as not to forget your name
Wrote in the palm of the hand the origin and destination of your journey
You are fear that reared up on its hind legs
And let its sideburns and beard grow
You are hoarse seeking the right word in the whirlwind of silence
Between your eyes' paths darkness thickens for you
And between your teeth laughter which you find harder and harder to
         remember
For its reins are not in your hands
You laugh in the direction in which others pull the moustache
Carry your soul in the nose while they teach you how to sneeze
You'll tie another knot one name in each moustache
Neither Relja to the Serbs nor Hariton to the Greeks.

Third Song

But I'm the one to whom others spit in the hand when he works
And in the plate when he eats
The one who failed to warm his chair
The eater of knives and darkness
From one mad rock to another I leap
While one leg wishes no good to the other
I eat with a penny under my tongue
With tears and sweat and I salt my bread
In one pocket wheat grows for me in the other grass
Rain falls in my bowl and snow in my bed
I'm the one who combs himself with a fork
The one who plants knives and fattens his teeth

Since spoons do not grow bigger while I eat
They gave me wine inside a bell
If I drink it doesn't toll if it tolls I don't drink.

Fourth Song
Rejoice bather between two waters
For you are the one who forgot where the earth's navel is
You stepped on someone's robe in the dark
They beat you by the clock and plant a hair in your egg
While you yawn into the flute
Steal God's days and devour them:
To the first that comes you bite off an ear or a finger
At night you are the one who practices gardening
You plow your shadow and water it with sweat
You planted the root of an ancient word
And grass grew on your tongue
Thus you guard yourself not to utter *above* or *below*
Nor *cold* nor *hot* nor *East* nor *West*
When you grow hoarse with your dumbness
You'll spit into the candle and die
Neither ours in what you have nor yours in what we have.

Fifth Song
But I'm the one who carries a garlic clove in the ear
My head in the sack my brain beyond the sea
I stuck a gold coin in my bread
And let the bread float down the river
I turned the eyes of rings in my hand and go begging
My river is full of apples my waters flower twice
My day breaks until noon from noon on it sets
Master of sundials and moon clocks
I pour water on unless the great royal highways

Disappear from under my feet
For the years wane behind the hills
And my day grows cold my honesty old
They've salted my fire domesticated my fork
And teach me to bring the moon rock in my teeth
While I piss in my shadow and make supper for my clock
Plant fish and mean to harvest hair
Neither a sackful of days nor handful of years
Sleep is my older brother and illness my older sister
Bite me in the tongue if they don't outlive me
And I neither sipped nor blew nor ate nor broke into crumbs.

Sixth Song

Rejoice singer of songs for the deaf
For you are the one for whom we stick a crown under the hat
They gave you two tamed shadows
To lie in one and cover yourself with the other
You answer to bread and water and travel blind
They strung your *gusla* with ravenous manes
They taught you our sorrow and weeping
Burdened the horse with the icon of Saint Paul
Whipped him hard under you
Alone ate the grass of forgetting that wipes out all memory
And thus forgot the name of their milk
And by what seed they were sown
We tell you—a careful manhunter of elusive dreams
Can even out of the night bring sweet water in his mouth
But you are the one whose tongue has a bad chill
Whose family name grows hoarse with silence
When you get thirsty you'll drink up the darkness
Die under a foreign fruit tree and with a foreign name
Neither a magus to yourself nor to us a prophet.

Seventh Song

Rejoice eleventh finger reckoner of stars
For you are the one exiled into the light
Your mind is made up with angelic speed
While the wings were given to you to catch him
We threw him on heaven's shores like a crown
To listen to the moon's breathing
Where he falls down we'll build a house
Go now and bring him back
In a sleeve full of moonlight
We are teaching you to bear God's beard
To crawl out among the stars
Like a worm from an iron walnut into the flesh of the wind
But you sit in your heart above all nights and fish
We teach you to spit at the point of galactic balance
Between the pull of the moon and the pull of the earth
But you've caught the mole of heavens
Sowed feathers in her back
And wait for the wings to sprout
You teach her to tell time
Terrestrial time makes her hiccup
Neither you last name's name nor your first name's nickname.

Eighth Song

But I'm the one from whom they stole a button from his trouser leg
The one who keeps a finger in the bottle instead of a cork
Priest of a god with two suns I bow down to two cats
And they teach me to steal my cap
Servant of two masters I stand on one leg
There where it thundered last year
I keep an eye on royal highways
Whether they join on the hill

With a wooden bell I count the horseman on this side
For the knowledge of those beyond the hill and vice versa
When I make an error confusion follows and they both run
But they stole a button from my trouser leg
And I keep the finger in the bottle instead of a cork
Neither tzar's own nor king's nor shepherd's nor hunter's dog.

Ninth Song

Rejoice mason of years
For you are the one who builds a house for your hours
Keeps night in the mouth and grazes the clouds with the eyes
They've cut your hair under the pot
In the shape of the Greek letter *omega*
And you don't know how to read it
Only paupers and lepers bow down to it
For you are the one who with an anchor plows islands in the sky
And gathers beautiful places into a column
A moon rock you've planted under the pillow
You weep with tears of wine and water it
One day and perhaps even earlier
A flying city will grow
Constantinople neither in heaven nor on earth
You'll lock it so the angels can't get in
Instead of icons you'll place all of us there
Let him who can't get in be envious
Of the one who can't come out
We'll pull your shadow from under your feet
Bury it in the water
You won't have a place to land if you return
Neither Relja to the Serbs nor Hariton to the Greeks.

Flying Temple

Gird your beard three times with a belt and light a stove
   in a ditch to boil us some wine.
A crossroad is before us, and like a black letter-carrying pigeon
Only the woods still guard this night. Put a swarm of bees
   under your hat and plant a grain of poppy
Under your tongue. The temples will not see

Were golden asses and horses horned as deers will take us.
When your heart spills a sweet word: Birds love to hover
   above water,
All trails will go on never to return to us. But you,
Hang the earring of hearing with its precious stone
   and weave a whip out of your hair.

Bring the knife in the bread: the sky will be full of birds
   and rivers of fish.
What songs are left we'll take to the oysters
   and arrange the mosaic in the sand,
For look, shadow and shade are abandoning the dead trees and soar.

On the stage the stargazing actors, magicians, and fiddlers,
Come out of their century without sadness. There, too,
Where graveyard into graveyard doesn't fall during the same matins

We'll lie under the tablet of flying temple, to lower
   for each other a dove for a pillow.

The Swing over the Calm Source of Our Names

Where do you go vision without me through my dreams
   following a miraculous sight although your eyes sleep?
My heart knows the reason for your weariness
   when at dawn you return to this world, your face
Washed before waking in a warm medicinal basin
   on the bottom of a cool spring
Where stars are farther than ever from their images.
   My heart knows it but won't tell me.

Why do you run like dogs ahead of my life,
   eyes, fighting over unknown things around one of its corners?
Does anyone attack you in forests that are still to come
And can I too drink from the drops you gather from tomorrow's rain?
If the eyes from another man's dream tear you to bits
   will I awake blind in the morning?

A little girl in white socks and in the swing of golden hair
   sways over your basin and the names that have drowned in it
Return to her from the healing waters as they evaporate,
But she doesn't understand them and plays with our
   precious names as she would with pebbles

Before she throws them back into the well. In vain you dive
   each night and bring them back changed into colors.
Throw them back. I no longer know the way from color to word.
My heart knows it but won't tell me and so now
   only that little girl in white socks

Can still help us, but she feels unable, or won't be their nurse.

IVAN V. LALIĆ

[1931–1996]

Lalić started publishing in 1952 and his first book, *A Child Once*, came out in 1955. Since then there have been many more books of poetry, all highly regarded, which have been translated into many languages, including English. Most of the poems here are taken from *Roll Call of Mirrors*, a selection of Lalić's poems published in 1988. He translated Hölderlin, Whitman, Dickinson, and many other American poets.

Love in July

I
Open this evening like a letter,
Its handwriting spotted with blood of birds
Devoured in the bright lava of the afternoon.

Open this evening like a rose,
That dust, that bronze, and that sweat on your skin,
That constellation that breathes.

Open this evening like a letter.
I'm hidden in its handwriting
Like a shadow in the still leaves of a cherry tree,
Or like noon in our blood.

Comes night grown over with rain and cherries,
And the wavering diamonds of sudden freshness.
Open this evening like a letter.

The date is illegible, time without beginning,
But the signature is clear:
                          I love.

II
The taste of the storm in the stalk of the invisible rose
That you twirl absentmindedly between your fingers.
Summer golden and dark.

But there's no wind, and the rain glitters
On your words like phosphorus
On the seams of the water.
Summer golden and dark.

The lightning that travels slower than memory
Will never again give us light in this place.

That lightning still buried in snows and flowers
In its journey around the year.

The taste of rain on your lips,
Summer golden and dark.

from Spring Liturgy for Branko Miljković

Tree in the wind remembered like a letter
In a word that will blaze like carbide.
Tree in the wind cast like lead
And printed in the sky already difficult to read.
Tree, bare marker of the earth in a windy landscape,
O deaf and mute tree between two fields of wheat,
Sign of maimed memory. In a forgotten place
The poem lives, fire burns, the sea has its origins
And the shape of the first tree in the raw air
Imitates the star of forgetting under its bark.
The world is visible where it returns from oblivion.
Tree in the wind, first letter of the cracked dawn.
The bird sleeps in the sea, the word in a well of a child's tears,
And still, a poem is a poem even when it's made of clay.

Believe me, fire is fire even without the deceptive spark.
In water, in sand, in loss, the fire arms itself.
The order of stars survives even after the planetariums are torn down,
Silence circles the poems and knots together the words.
This reality is springlike, it repeats itself,
Before the flash of forgetting it narrows like an eye,
Ceases like the sea before the deaf citadel of land,
But at every land's edge the sea wakes
Already announced by the damp wind, the membrane
Of the slumbering vision bursts. O tree in the wind,
The fire dawns on the edge of the first leaf
That no longer remembers that there is neither a beginning
Nor an end, and so marvels only at its shape.
Tree in a wind, letter in a brief word written by the passionless law,
Tree that stutters with arms full of living rain.

Beauty endures. It matters not whether it remembers,
The road continues past the broken rails.
In truth, there's no death. In truth, the bird flies
And the great delusion is a body laid out in the morgue.
Tree in the wind, you who are the bare marker of the mighty earth,
You open your leaves like a flag. You're the sentry
Of a battle already decided. Your root touches
The cornerstone of that nourishing oblivion.
The air changes your pronunciation
And every springtime proves once again the Mediterranean.
The sea awakes itself again behind the deafest rocks.
The bird inscribes its song around the blazing nest.
Tree in the wind, o word of the wise moment,
Look, beauty is returning like pillage,
And the sea glitters with stars, stars, stars!

Insomnia

One more hour to remember, one less sip
In the glass of water on the table.
                              Mother,
How strangely the paths fork in your garden!
At their every turn,
Fewer and fewer opportunities to solve this night.
It frightens me, my future face
In the mirror when the day breaks,

As if already I've stood in that very spot
Which the snake yields, and then slithers off.
She gave me permission to envision the door
Partly open with love, for her to visit us
And stay—perhaps in this space
Which can fit inside a word, the moment I shut my eyes,
Uselessly . . .
                   How to step forth
With my heart into the heart of the riddle?
The morning scatters your garden
With hands of cold fire which I glimpse already
Behind the curtain. The stars have almost trickled out in the west
Like grains of sand down the sides of clepsydra,
And the pain of that image eases,
Heals like a severed hand without a scar—
But sleep is not solution, it is a mercy . . .
How strangely the paths fork in your garden,
Mother.
          A serpent's tongue flickering
On my eyelash in the moment
Before I drift off to sleep.

Roll Call of Mirrors

Count the mirrors, count the walled-in windows,
The dangerous backdrops of air
Where the double breathes confident and slow
From time immemorial.
                              In the mirror, at night,
Strike the brief yellow life of a match,
You'll glimpse the threat in the wound of dark
That heals quickly—scarless,
                              and then, under the fingertips,
The dry ice of Lethe without a crack or hope.

Count, appraise the danger.
The story goes that someday there'll be
A clank at the bottom of the mirror
Before the final exit of the double
                              in the instant
Before the earth's double heart stops
Divided by the knife of memory—
                              like a ripe fruit.

Broadcast

The image flickers, a firefly
Pinned by an invisible pin, lengthened
Into the eye-nerve, weary from paying attention.
Distorted voice, erratic, disappearing
Like a sunken stream in caverns below hearing.
Dismembered words, magnetized by that chill,
Link each other in stubborn meaninglessness.
We focus the image in our memory:
                         the traffic of consonants . . .
Agreement about cease-fire—
                         then a blank.
The missing sequence replaced by a white glow
Of a sky hardened into a wall. Here
                              the voice returns
And quarrels with the image of a great city
Already breaking up from left to right,
Crumbling like an accelerated Babylon
In a defeat of lines that fail to obey
The order to remain vertical.
                         Here the voice fades.
We remember half a sentence, the context vague.
An unusually important broadcast, they say,
Last before the long loveless night,
And no one who remembers anymore
How the interference and poor reception began.

Voices of the Dead

1

Voices of the dead. They are not dead. Who hears
The dead? Rain on the bronze gates of the morning,
The freshness of wild gardens keeping doves
In the cobwebs of roses. I was that emptiness between them.

I was on a bank of a river lost for days, hours.
It doesn't matter. In time beyond this time.
And the river is wide, river from the blood of ancestors.
How to swim up its stream? Who has reached its mouth?

O dead ones, by this river I found a roofless house,
House left in a hurry and a thin thread of smoke
Woven into mist that grows thicker and thicker.

House uncompleted. Then winter began.
A window frightened by the strength of a storm woke me up.
Voices of the dead. They are not dead. Who hears them?

2

In the night a distant fire blazes. Then another.
Butterflies of flame settle the rim of the night.
Third fire. Soon, a clean line of fire
Completed. Ring of sleep. Nobody gets through.

Chestnuts shake off their leaves in fear.
Men say: Autumn. Melisa, it is the camp
Of a great dead army, settled on a distant hill.
Alone, breathless and troubled, I listen for the bugle.

Instead of ringing brass, I hear early snows
Falling in empty woods. The fires remain.
When the earth smooths a wrinkle on its forehead,

Entire towns collapse. The fires remain.
Ring around sleep. Has anyone heard the bugle?
Bugle beyond silence and the silence stronger.

3
Voices of the dead remain beyond my hearing.
That too is part of the game, Melisa, that too is law
Mixed in my wine, kneaded in my bread,
Carved with a red knife into a nailed door

Toward which I keep looking since they lead on.
Voices of the dead are not the buzzing of your bees
That melt on scented leaves like drops of gold
When I follow them: they are not in rustling firs

Grown on bloodied thighs of mountains.
They are beyond this game, beyond this instant.
A path leads to your garden, Melisa. It can be taken,

Armed with what I don't posses. But without a knife,
Without a cry. No one dead or alive can help me.
O terrible beauty of the game without a go-between.

4
Voices of the dead remain. Distant voices. Who hears
The dead? Perhaps the color of old gold
And the foam of dark sea. Perhaps like a storm
Lacking space. Perhaps hushed after an illness.

Unknown. It doesn't matter. Perhaps soiled by war,
Dust. Or with a quiet noise like a seashell
Placed against the ear on a burning summer afternoon.
It doesn't matter. Voices beyond this game. Kindred words.

The buzzing of the spindle in the fairy lullaby
From a pure age. Dream disguised into an event.
Voices of the dead. Still they are not dead.

I lie in the night. Awake. Quiet. They are quieter.
I fall asleep and dream of drums. Ancient drums.
Great dark drums broken and left in the rain.

Raven's Monologue

The dove, I think, is more suited
To do that errand, to bring back news
In her small, weary beak
Already thickened into a symbol:
A twig of hope for the painter
Who's making the peace poster.
That's why I chose absence
Now that the water gates of heaven,
The fountains of the abyss,
Are shut off. I chose a clear mind.
Before me, the Flood.
On my dark wing I bear the sun,
Severely mind my own business,
Expertly peck in the mud
The sinner's eyes. And caw.
They'll paint me on coats of arms,
Standing in the snow
Black like a letter.
They'll teach me to say Nevermore.
I'll be famous. The dove, however,
Seems to be made for this job.
In her image let hope grow a feather
So that in mine, horror may preen its image.

First Actor to Hamlet

Okay, Prince, we understand the instructions
How to put your mousetrap together.
Everything has to serve a purpose. We won't
Saw the air with our hands. As for passion,
It will remain intact like Christ's mantle.
We'll make ourselves, as you desire, a mirror
In which vice can see its spitting image.
The King's heart will skip a beat.
                        Torches, torches, torches!
Yes, Prince, that will be a perfect trap
To catch beasts the way mathematics catches
The star's next position. You'll be pleased.

But wait! What shadows cast by what actors
Are enacting for you now some other play?
The mirror is fogged, the gestures are unclear,
The prompter cannot be heard.
                        You rise
Obediently and confidently like a sleepwalker
While behind the sets four captains
Play cards, wait for a sign from the stage manager
Who we've heard is getting ready to journey to Poland.

We'll incorporate that play, too, into our own
As if it were another stone in the ring of your killer.

Addressing the Comet

You thunder in my spirit as you approach again,
You twofold anguish of the century
Making a double stitch along its path.
Long-tailed fire thirty times observed
Since Aegean night when Herodotus perhaps
Saw you and kept quiet;
                           fire that sings
The length of a training field where the skill
Of punctual return is practiced,
The skill of some uncalled-for constancy
Venerated by tradition. Fire beloved
By something indescribable that waits for you here
And then sees you off into the measured abyss.

Why do you return? What is it that you wish
Repeatedly to be a witness to? The one who
Got entangled in the web of equations
Staring from the zero meridian into the horror vacui,
Measured only the snakeskin,
Measured the direction and the length of the track
Of someone's steps in the sand—
                           while you went on singing
About the love of the one who walks the sand.

Who walks the sand and then halts
To start a fire of soaked twigs
While at the other bank, at nightfall,
That fire, distant and low above the water
Narrows to a point, a newborn star.

As for what you recognize and come back for,
The historian doesn't know, preoccupied as he is by purpose.
O fire that sings, what do you witness
On what might be your last return?

ALEKSANDAR RISTOVIĆ

[1933–1994]

Born in Čačak, Ristović studied Serbian language and literature and taught school for many years at the elementary and high-school level in his hometown. His first book of poems was published in 1959. Since then there have been over twenty, as well as a novel, a dream book, and numerous essays. In 1989 Charioteer Press brought out a book of his poems, *Some Other Wine and Light,* and in 1999 a large selection of his poetry, *Devil's Lunch,* was published by Faber in England.

Untitled

Time of fools is coming.
Time of the fairground tent,
and the blasphemer with a funny face.

Time of the peacock quill,
the quill that glides from right to left
over the upside-down paper.

Time when you won't be able to lift your little finger
without dipping it into something
they call indecent.

Time of fools is coming,
time of the know-nothing teacher
and the book that can't be opened at either end.

The Law

Put aside the papers, your Honor,
and take note of the one who has entered your chamber
on the day before the main hearing.

She says she's about to bear her brother's child;
artfully, in the meantime, concealing her swollen belly
with a richly colored cape.

A dog sits before your door,
a dog who belongs to the unfortunate one with holes in her shoes.
It whines and rattles its chain.

Do her the favor she asks of you.
Enter a paragraph next to a number
not to be found in the book with metal covers.

She'll exit as she came, bowing low,
while tucking her tiny hands
in the folds of her woolen cape.

Flirting with a Pig

Come to me pig, you who dress yourself as a courtier while still
    wallowing in the mud,
come to me with your small eyes averted.
I have understanding for your embarrassment and for your vanity.

It's not right for a poet to like the same things you do,
but there's something dear to me in your debauchery,
to which you yield with permanent ambivalence.

Still, the devil waits for you in the slaughterhouse.
He has fat fingers, a sheepskin coat, and fine cutting instruments.
He stands with legs spread apart in the middle of a large room, wearing
    rubber boots and playing with knives.

In the meantime, his helper rinses the wooden pail
and watches the boss's daughter climb down the ladder,
lifting her skirt so that her pink soles and shins show.

Come to me, pig, mistress of the bog,
I'd like to whisper sweet nothings into your wide ear before they lead
    you away,
by turns throwing curses and praises upon you.

Gingerbread Heart

Make me a long coat of heavy cloth, tailor—
the kind the wind won't thread—
and of a dark color,
so that no one will notice the cigarette ashes.

Make it of the same material as the dark trousers,
to last as long as I want them to,
wearing them to visit many cities, villages, and other out-of-the-way places.

Make me a dark vest, O tailor,
in which to sit at a feast table surrounded by happy faces,
with a rich man's rose in one of its buttonholes.

Make me a dark jacket, tailor,
with wide and deep pockets in which to clench my fists
while watching the one they're dragging from my table into the bushes,
which then began to shake after a few moments.

Despair

You opened the matchbox.
There was a single match left.
You took it out, so that now
the box was empty.
You put three ladybugs in it.
With that one match you set
the box on fire,
and while it burned,
giving off just a little smoke,
you turned toward me,
to laugh in my face!

Old Motif

For whom are you intended, wine in the corked bottle
on a white tablecloth,
next to some swaying flowers,
while a young girl sweeps the still-empty room?

You'll untie the tongue of the silent one,
make the fool into a wise man,
and to the weakling you'll give courage
to act on his secret desire.

Out of the wise man you'll make a foolish one
who squanders his wealth among the much pampered servants and flunkies
and who promises the big-breasted cashier
a house with pine needles on the floor.

Perhaps you'll turn the head of a beautiful woman
so that she'll quit the table for one of the upstairs rooms
followed by some worthless fellow
who makes up verses with only one thing in mind.

For a time, perhaps, you'll change the old man into that youth in the tavern
who sings and taps his foot,
while frequently visiting the lavatory to flirt with the one
busy counting the small coins in a cigar box.

For whom are you intended, wine in the corked bottle?
Through whose veins will you send your merry little flame,
making him see the most ordinary things
in many strange and unaccustomed ways?

Outhouse

Through a crack on the right
you can see the red rooster,
and through the one on the left,
with a bit of effort,
you can see the table,
the white cover
and a bottle of wine.
Behind your back, if you turn,
you'll make out the sheep
trying to fly with their woolen wings.
And through the heart-shaped
hole in the door,
someone's cheerful face
watching you shit.

Monastic Outhouse

In the back of the nunnery
there's a small outhouse
with a half-open door and evening visitors.
While one is inside,
another waits her turn
with her nose in the book.
And while the first one exits,
straightening her robes,
her face almost radiant,
the other one steps in,
peeks into the spotless hole,
trembling with terror
that what lies at the bottom
may leap into her face
and leave a mark on her flushed cheek
in the shape of a devil's cross.

Out in the Open

While crossing a field,
someone who in that instant
is preoccupied with thoughts of suicide,
is forced by nature's call
to delay the act,
and so, finds himself enjoying
some blades of grass
from a squatting position,
as if seeing them for the first time
from that close,
while his cheeks redden,
and he struggles to pull a sheet of paper
out of his pocket
with its already composed
farewell note.

Maids

One is in the cellar,
the other one is in the attic.
One carries a lamp and a platter into the dark room for guests sensitive
    to cold,
the other sits behind the house
staring at the moon rising over the nearby trees.
One travels by the village bus forty kilometers through a snowstorm,
the other tries to light a fire while sitting on the iron bed next to her mother,
    who is already seeing angels like hundreds and hundreds of fireflies.
One weeds the onions, waters the garden, chases a chicken,
the other stands by the window holding before her face a rose-colored leaf
    that gives off no scent.
One is at the table where she diligently polishes dishes, knives, spoons,
    and forks,
while a bee (which flew in through the window) in vain tries to find a way out
    bumping into the curtain and the pane,
and the other one smokes strong tobacco
with some good-for-nothing from the neighborhood, constantly raising and
    lowering her eyes.
But soon the night will be here,
and both of them will find themselves in their own beds,
one with a novel on her knees lit by the table lamp,
the other one already dreaming the first dream of that night:
    in which she sees the seashore, the thin line of waves,
    and herself losing pieces of her clothing one by one,
    while walking with greater and greater speed toward
    someone whose face is hidden by a shadow of an almost
    imaginary rose.

About Death and Other Things

How strange will be my death, of which I've been thinking since childhood:
A sedentary old man leaving a small-town library
leans to one side and eventually collapses on the lawn.

I've every reason to believe that I'll experience what the others have
    experienced
while I climb the stairs carrying my supper in a plastic bag,
not even turning to look at the one who in that moment descends curly-
    haired and wearing a party dress.

It could be an ordinary death on a train:
a man who carefully studies the fields and hills in snow,
shuts his eyes, folds his hands in his lap, and no longer sees what only
    a moment ago he admired.

I'm trying to remember other possibilities and so, here I am once again,
disguised as myself in a small, merry company,
where, after emptying my glass, I fall on the floor laughing, and pulling
    after me the tablecloth with the vase full of roses.

My death, of course, would have a spiritual meaning
in some mountain sanatorium for the insane
where croaking we complain to each other in beds with freshly changed
    sheets.

It could happen that I'll die in some way very different from the one
    I anticipate:
in the company of my wife and daughter, surrounded by books,
while outside a neighbor is trying to start a car that the night has surprised
    with snow.

Dead Leaves

Danton is waiting to die
but the day won't break.
His vest is full of lice
and he has rain in his boots.
On his face there are already signs
of his exceptional destiny.
He watches me from a great distance
walk under the trees
and gather dead leaves
with a long stick ending in a spike.

Strange Students

The buzzing in the next room
must come from tiny insects
who recently took up residence there.
For the time being, they're invisible.

In the evening, as I listen to them,
I have the impression that they're memorizing
in concert a particular subject,
most likely something to do with botany.

Once in a while, they come to a sudden stop,
as if to hear their teacher speak:
his sternness, that they find so frightening,
cloaked in silence.

When they resume, it's on a higher note,
as if now competing with each other.
I'm beginning to recognize certain groupings
and among them, one or two gifted individuals.

And, of course, a few real dummies, too.

JOVAN HRISTIĆ

[1933–2002]

Hristić studied philosophy, and after many years of work-
ing in publishing, he taught at the drama school in Belgrade,
where he was born. His first book, *The Diary of Ulysses*,
came out in 1954, and his *The Alexandrian School* in 1963.
He wrote five plays, a study of Chekhov, a book of essays, and
translated T. S. Eliot and Cavafy. Hristić was also a drama
critic.

To Phaedrus

This, too, I want you to know, my dear Phaedrus,
We lived in hopeless times. Out of tragedy
We made comedy; out of comedy tragedy.

But the true seriousness, measure, wise exaltation,
And exalted wisdom always eluded us. We were
On no-man's-land, neither being ourselves

Nor being someone else, but always a step or two
Removed from what we are and what we ought to be.

O my dear Phaedrus, while you stroll
With noble souls on the island of the blessed,
Recall at times our name too.

Let its sound resound in the resonant air.
Let it ascend toward that heaven it could never reach,
So that in your conversation, at last, our souls may find peace.

That Night They All Gathered on the Highest Tower

That night they all gathered on the highest tower:
Astronomers, mathematicians, and one of the magi from Syria
To read in the stars the glory of the King of Kings,
And demonstrate his immortality with the aid of geometry.

Just before dawn, they nodded their heads in accord
With one another's interpretations. The answer of the stars
Was positive. The trumpets announced
The glory of the King of Kings to the rising sun.

In the palace, at the table set for the feast, they were awaited
By the one to whom the stars gave their word tonight,
And whose future now overflowed like new wine
Which in the golden chalices awaited the toasts.

Only some youth who had recently mastered geometry
Was not fully convinced by what was read in the stars,
For the stars always give their answer to mortals
But to what question, only they themselves know.

A Sentimental Voyage around My Room

Slowly, the summer was ending with a shower. We were
Not given to conclude our travels. We lingered forgetting
The strength of the beginning in the vain happiness of the end.

I was meeting myself again in the same silence and the sea,
That future life, slept in the anemic sunlight
While the old poison slowly filled my whole bloodstream.

Beginning in the same room, and in the same one ending,
While the same battles covered the walls like shadows
Awaiting their wings. Slowly, the summer was ending with a shower.

Eyes of some future morning, forgive us who will never
Know about you. Forgive our rooms, while the old poison already
Went on slowly filling our whole bloodstream.

Evening Quiet

You in evening doorways, in half-lit streets,
Next to side entrances, next to walls
Of red brick and broken glass,
Who embraced, dream about moonlight
On a cat vanished among the curtain folds,
Or in the barking of a dog,
You two, you two alone in the dark, alone
And sleepless against a light pole without a light.

You two somewhere in a park, on a path
Beyond leaves and clouds, between two rains,
Between two winds on a bench wet with tears,
Owning nothing but a small room
With an iron cot and books on a chair,
And a cold sun beyond the yellow pane.
You who are lonely even while embracing
Hard enough to squeeze out the very wing of solitude.

While you whisper the few words found
In these moments of accidental tenderness,
Words said many times already
Wherever there was a moon and the night,
While you walk the city streets
Deserted after the last performances
In movie theaters, walk embraced
This wet street, more unreal than a dream
With your eyes shut and your fingers idle.

Do you hear the steps of someone behind you?
Do you hear his words among your whispers?
Do you feel his touch among your touches?
For always when you walk alone thinking
That there's no one here to throw a pebble of his voice
In the darkened water of the silence between you,
Remember always the one who stubbornly
Walks behind your back calling on you to wake up.

The Tragedy Is Over

The tragedy is over. Blind Oedipus exits
into his darkness, into our darkness.
The chorus remains behind on the square
to mumble a few additional verses
and then disperses homeward, where already one can smell
the evening meals being cooked.

That's our moment. The curtain hasn't yet
been lowered as we step on the stage:
the columns of the palace are suddenly of cardboard,
the blood that drew so much pity and fear
is spilling from the bottle with colored water,
while with wooden swords we begin our play.
Everything you saw we'll make you see once more:
Oedipus will again answer the riddle and gouge his eyes out,
Jocasta will scream in the wings, the messenger
will arrive and announce the latest horrors,
and the blood will flow.

In a pause, between two verses, while the costumes
and scenery are changed, in the silence and darkness,
perhaps at the very end when the sets are removed,
and the last lights are being turned off,
the scream of Oedipus, whose long shadow
has, too, disappeared behind a hill,
will once again be heard.

But only for a moment. We will continue our play
happy that we were called to come out on the stage
and display our art before the lights were out.

In the Big Library

In the big library scholars sit and read books.
I sit among them, but do not know why.

From time to time one of them dozes off,
And then gets up to have a cup of coffee.

I'm staying since I'm the only one among them who doesn't know
Why he reads the books piled up before him on the table.

Outside the sun is shining, squirrels hop on the lawns
And climb trees. I sit and read.

One must do something. People pass on the street.
They've got things to do. I read and read
Since I've got nothing else to do, and time is slow to pass.

Barbarians

The messengers finally arrived and said:
The barbarians are coming.
They're getting ready to welcome them in the city.
Elated young men already cheer their names
And hurry to celebrate the new gods.
Haven't the poets said those people were a kind of solution?
Now they write poems in their glory
Waiting for the day when they'll declaim them in public
While the admiring, heavily armed barbarians
Applaud them and learn their verses by heart.
Already they see their poems in large letters
Hung in the porticoes of the temples
From which the impotent deities have been evicted,
And libraries full of their books
Taking the place of stories that no longer speak to anyone.

Still, the poets know they'll be the first to hang in public,
Together with the young men who hurried to open the gates
And admit into the city those they eagerly awaited,
Since barbarians are barbarians and are no solution at all.

In a Dark Hour

In a dark hour (there are more and more of them now),
He sits alone afraid to turn on the lights within reach of his hand
In a room that the darkness is slowly filling,
Like smoke that till then had lingered in the gardens
Where they burn the newly fallen leaves waiting for the first frost.

In a moment now steps will be heard.
Some god is coming to close the door
To one more room in his life
He will never again enter.

He waits for the sound of steps to cease.
Then he rises, turns on the light
And stands motionless in the middle of the room,
The last one that remains to him, full of books and papers,
And knows that nothing of what he desired will happen,
Now that what he feared most is already happening.

BRANKO MILJKOVIĆ

[1934–1960]

As a child in Niš, Milkjović witnessed two massacres dur-
ing the war. He studied literature and philosophy at the
university, translated French symbolist poetry and Russian
poetry, and started publishing early. In 1960 he moved to
Zagreb, where he hung himself in February 1961, a week
after writing a letter to a periodical renouncing all his
poetry. Since his death, his brief life has become as legend-
ary as Sylvia Plath's.

Shepherd's Flute

Sweet fever of wind-troubled flowers,
You feel it coming. Plants, you bend again
On the trail of the drunken south and vanished summer.
Hurry, praise the world in a song.
Repent the day because of ungrateful flesh
Which gives back to the sun a shadow
And spoils the song. Give the solitary man
A bird. Under the empty heavens
The falconers cry. Call back into the legend
The phantoms from the hills.
Let all the senses touch in a song
So that they may not lose freshness
In the night of the body. Let there be
Loss and less of the visible so that memory
May reign supreme. Empty what's in my lap
And take my heart. Hurry, sing the eternal recurrence,
And fool our misfortune.
Open the city gates, seduce the bird.
Under the empty heavens the falconers cry.

Sun

This aimless drifting will conclude
with the sun. I feel the south
stirring in my heart. A spark
of tiny noon mocking inside a stone

that will light up my starry bloodstream.
Till then let everything depend on song.
I need no other consolation. That life
mocks the threat of some black and venomous essence.

No, that voyage will conclude with venom.
Another cosmos will again give us life.
Blind and dark-hearted, say the true word:
In the stone sleeps the dim sun that'll give us light.

Do you hear my starry bloodstream!
I repeat, another cosmos will give us life
blind and dark-hearted till the sun speaks
above the threat of some black, venomous essence.

Ballade

Wisdom, innocently the sun rises,
I no longer have the right for simple words!
My heart grows dim, my eyes burn.
Sing wonderful old men while over our heads
The stars burst like metaphors.
What is lofty, vanishes; what is low, rots.
Bird, I'll make you speak but give back
The flame you borrowed. Don't blaspheme the ashes.
In a stranger's heart we heard our heart beat.
To sing and to die is the same thing.

Sun is a word unable to throw light.
Conscience doesn't know how to sing for it dreads
Its own raw emptiness. Thieves of visions,
Eagles, peck at me from within. I stand
Nailed to a rock that does not exist.
We've signed in lieu of stars the night's
Deceit, so much darker. Remember
That fall into life was a proof of your embers.
When ink ripens into blood everyone will know,
To sing and to die is the same thing.

Wisdom, the stronger one will be the first to yield.
Only rogues know what poetry is.
Thieves of fire, not one of you is the least lovable,
Tied to the mast of a ship followed
Under water by a song more dangerous than reality,
The blackened-out sun in the ripe orchard will know
How to take the place of a kiss that soothes the ashes.
But, no one after us will have the strength
To endear himself to a nightingale
When to sing and to die is the same thing.

Life is deadly but it has a way of surmounting death.
A fatal illness will be named after me.
We've suffered so much. Now the domesticated hell
Sings. Let the heart not hesitate,
To sing and to die is the same thing.

The Sea before I Start Dreaming

The world vanishes slowly. We all study
The deceitful time on the wall. Let us go!
The borders within which we live
Are not the borders within which we die.
Dull-edged night, dead bodies,
The heart is dead but the abyss remains.
Tonight the water wants to drink itself
To the bottom and then to rest.

Travel while there's still a world and knowledge.
Dust will make you beautiful. You'll know the ashes and the light.
Go blind on the road you're walking, but remember:
The sun is false, but the path is true.
Let merchants of time sail with wax in their ears.
Listen bravely how the deserts sing
While white stars kneel before the locked sea.
There's still strength in you to crucify yourself.

Emptiness, how puny the stars are!
Your dream lacks a body, your night lacks nightliness,
An adjective of a pure stone full of praise.
That which I see, is it mine or your power?

Transparent enclosure that the glow overcomes,
Deserted transparency that terrifies me,
Your flower is the only star above the city,
Your hopelessness is of pure gold.

The world vanishes slowly, the sad world.
Who'll bury our hearts and bones
There where memory doesn't reach
Where days do not multiply and repeat us!
Pull my tongue out and stick a flower in its place:

My wanderings are beginning. Stop the words.
Tomorrow even a coward will be able to do
What today only the just and brave can,
Who in the space between us and the night
Discovered the reasons of a glorious and different love.

The world vanishes. We believe fiercely
In the thought no one has thought yet,
In the empty place, in the sea foam when with emptiness
The water mingles and then roars.

Black Horseman

Wild night bitter and vertical
like a fence a black horseman advances
to contrive a plot with roads
night closed tightly into a fist

His voice will empty the audible space
his words will wake nightmares
on the bottom of his black eye lies
a dog ready to bark at any heaven

Black horseman imagined by the bitter
wild night which the horseman carried
down frightening roads that quarreled
and parted to four corners of the world

Black horseman no one knows
whose name the winds scattered
black horseman the only one to seek us
beyond ourselves and slay our absence

O terrible thought of the black horseman
when in the morning we got up bloody
our throats cut our arms severed
powerless to shout and grasp

O terrible thought of the black horseman
seen for the first time on Red Baniji
who imprisoned in our skull
still gallops from its front to its back

Miners

They descend into hell after injustice
On which it is possible to warm oneself.

Agon

While the river banks are quarreling,
The waters flow quietly.

from **In Praise of Plants**

V
I know your root
But what is the grain from which your shadow grows
Vegetal beauty so long invisible
                  in the seed
You found under the earth my headless body
                  which dreams a true dream
Stars lined up in a pod
All that is created with song and sunlight
Between my absence and your herbal
                  ambitions of night
That make me needed even when I'm absent
Green microphone of my subterranean voice
                  weed
Growing out of hell since there is no other sun
                  under the earth
O plant where are your angels resembling
                  insects
And my blood which weaves oxygen and time

Sea without Poets

You wait for a right moment
To attune yourself to words
But there is no such poet
Nor a word fully free
O bitter and blind sea
In love with shipwreck

Sleepers

Awake I steal what they dream.

Everyone Will Write Poetry

a dream is an old and forgotten truth
that no one knows how to verify anymore
now strangeness sings like sea and troubles
east is west of the west that lie is quickest
now wisdom sings and birds of my neglected illness
a flower midway between ashes and scent
those who refuse to live through love
and the lovers who turn back the clock
the garden whose scents the earth doesn't recognize
the earth that remains faithful to death
since this world is not the sun's only worry

but the day will come
there where the heart was the sun will shine
human language won't have a word left
that will refuse to sing
everyone will write poetry
the truth will be in every word
in a place where the poem is most beautiful
the one who first started to sing
will withdraw so that others may continue

I accept the great ambition of future poetries:
an unhappy man cannot be a poet
I accept the verdict of the singing multitude
he who doesn't know how to listen to a poem
will listen to a storm

but:

will freedom know how to sing
the way the slaves sang about it?

LJUBOMIR SIMOVIĆ

[1935–]

Simović was born in Užice and studied literature and philosophy at the University of Belgrade. He is a successful playwright as well as poet. Since his first book, *Slavic Elegies,* was published in 1958, there have been a number of other collections and a volume of selected poems.

Epitaph

To the chimney a horns of a bull
To the window a lamb's skin
To the tomb a raven's feathers
To the kettle a cloud and smoke
To the hearth a bit of grass
To the autumn rain and stars
To the cloud a king's galleon
And to me through the autumn air
Over my only fire
A shovel full of black earth.

One Evening

I was a belfry and blizzard of birds,
and ramparts, and the chalice thrown from the ramparts; now it's in the sea
    and the sea is in it;
I was a king cleaning the boots of the bootmaker,
I was a pigeon on a marble helmet,
a square and the ropemaker weaving the rope
and the criminal hung by that rope.

I was a soldier raising his glass like a flag
and another, in the stable,
on top of a nurse who embraces him fainting.
In the grass, with flowers high as the horse's belly,
I was the horse and its rider, night through which they ride,
I was the fields, the messenger and his evil tidings.

I was everywhere and everyone, seeking how to throw off my back
these worries and animals, the violence of fear and flowers,
evil and the inclination to evil:
                            but early one sleepless
evening, before a storm, in western Serbia, I saw
great flights of birds which as they rose from a tree
made it seem as if the tree had disappeared.

Traveling Star

I
Is anyone waiting for you at the end of the road?
Is the sky empty without man?

Or are you dark because you know
Of an even darker sun on which it's winter?

The gloom of the day that will not break
And how much ash remains from a single sun?

II
Is your glitter your speech? Did you shine
When they hung you by the tongue?

When my head fell in the mud,
You sent me greeting from the heavenly gallows.

And while the executioner wove the rope,
What is it that I understood in your glow?

So I keep silent before men who offer me bread,
And before judges ready to forgive me.

Notation in Gold

Among bloody candles I welcomed winter 1254.
Every night, to the chorus of wolves and blizzards,
my vigil lasted as long as the path of the flame
from top to bottom of the candle, when with crow's
feather I wrote the pages of monastic chronicle
for the year 1235 of our Lord.

In this small cell
I recognize summer by dust, winter by snow dust
sifted through narrow cracks.

The candle above my blinded eyes, knotted
like a finger of a leper with sharp nails of its flame,
already for many years points to heaven and reminds me.

Over my head, the bells sway
large like golden haystacks,
once long ago in the village of Volujci.

I dream I do not exist, I dream that someone
dreams of me and that the dawn is approaching,
and that the time is coming for him to awake.

Epitaphs from Karansko Cemetery

Here rests Tiosav
son of Miljka and Stamena
evening wind circles the candle
chases its shadow around it
the wheat has grown to the stars
the evening descends between tombs
here rests Tiosav buried with his shepherd's flute
here rests dead
Tiosav who wanted to live even
turned into a frog forgive him Lord even
turned into a green tree

    Refrain

    oi cloudy wind flies up into mist of warm swamps
    a single ancient star is creating all this confusion
    oi stop saying no to this bird falling down
    into this sunlit flame into the head of King Lazarus

Stanoje two months old
sleeps in a cradle of soil
nobody remembers him
born at the end of autumn died at the beginning of winter
darling among the dead
neither friends nor enemies remember him
his weeping cannot be told
his mound cannot be jumped over or avoided
his mound slowly turns into a dirt road
in a small hell of lit candles
over his grave it is dark

oi cold wind flies up into mist of warm swamps
a single ancient star is creating all this confusion
see the bird falling down from this scented sky
into this sunlit flame into the skull of King Lazarus

Koviljka daughter of Milisav and Stojanka
lived sixteen years
died on Ivan's Day
wreaths of birds break open in the sky
a mongrel loiters around the grave covered with flowers
a young man and a girl sleep naked on a hill
scented by the air of pine trees but the cross
spreads its arms and won't let us go further
neither into the forest nor
into the river nor into
the air

Refrain

oi blue wind flies up into mist of warm swamps
this starry morning is creating all this confusion
oi stop scream no to this bird falling down
into this sunlit flame into the tomb of King Lazarus

Dirge

Lit candles like spears
stuck, oi, into smoking
furrows. Over the body of hemp,
air deep to the morning star.
Above my head wax candles rustle
on my coffin apples tumble.

Crucifixion

Crucified Jesus on a yellow cross
Washed down by cold rain
Spreads his arms wide
As if playing the accordion.

He bends his ear down to the instrument
Better to hear its sound
Unaware the passing tinker took it
When he went by cold and hungry.

They all abandoned him, haughtily,
The revelers, the dancers
Only sparrows, crickets, and snowflakes
Still dance around him.

The cross is at the crossroads
Where the village road meets the country road.
If you hear music, stop and listen!
It's true, you can hear the music!

Curses

1
May the wind extinguish everything for you
except the candle on your grave.

May you not run away from the ax,
or the cannon.

May you not have fish in Fishville,
a bull in Bullsville,
nor a single sheep in Sheepsville.

May you be afraid to meet your brother
without a knife.

May you move from your house to the cemetery.

May you find neither a root nor a leaf.

May you stir with a right hand
the soup made with the left hand.

2
May you buy a hat
and have nothing to put it on.

May your wife knead dust,
rain's bread dough.

May your hair give you the slip,
your flesh too.

May you raise in vain your chin
above the flood.

May you breathe only as much
as your suffering requires.

3
May a man in armor await you
wherever you go.

May he ride into your wheat,
into your bed,
into your church.

May your kin rise against you.

All hounds on your trail!
All evils on what you hold dear!

May evil not touch you
until you raise your knife.

4
If in a stranger's eye
you didn't put the sun out.

If in the hour of the wolf
you didn't call out like a wolf.

May sun shine for you out of the wind,
out of your brother,
and a fish in the brook,
the oak tree, the unexpected guest.

With wheat up to your waist
and clear sky spreading,
with your arm around your wife

may you watch the back
of the flood.

Breakfast

Didn't I say last night it will snow?

What else would there be but snow?
I no longer wait for the rustle of wings,
or some dove to make my heart leap
and shine its light on me.

Snow has hatched in every den and lair
putting out every fire.
The snow: our key and lock.
I woke in my bed as if in another world,
as if in a drift of snow.
The three hills were all white.

I put on my cold boots, made a fire,
cut three rashers of bacon into the skillet
by the window where it's starting to snow again.
The bacon sizzles. I break an egg.
In the room the shadows of jackdaws fly to and fro.

I rejoice because of the egg.

IVAN GADJANSKI

[1937–]

Born in Jaša Tomić, Gadjanski studied classical languages, Balkan history, and culture at various European universities and at Columbia University in New York. He is a highly respected, experimental, and erudite poet. His first book of poetry was published in 1975; five other collections have followed.

Voyvodina

for a long time I've been searching for words
when the sun sets I expect to find them
but all I find is earth and grass

for a long time I've been searching for the authentic
white stone under the bird's wing
and always

> in the long long noon
> it's dawn again
> yellow light
> the sun is blazing
> the wind has stopped
> the bird is gone
> no bird is there

only history in its ocher silhouettes
animas of earth and wind
fly by gently with our memories
through geobiopsychic molds
playing with bright traces
with the hard chromatic writing of the stars' captured glitter
with the smell of honey
dry mud green black white

a snake-headed wind helen's brother
draws out the smooth whiteness of morning
across the old land of scythians
with so much variety as in things that stick in memory
images of the future on the dusty reliefs of the past
revealing dirty ochre on the boy's knees
and on the trapezoid banks of the great whirlpool the elusive cloud of the
    lazy deer
spins cantabile the milky truth

weaves blades of water weeds
in the tangled grass the snake easily touches the clay

      we bought white gravel for our garden
      and imported persian roses
      persian cats
      a persian czar
      we even got a white horse from vienna
      for our parade carriage zum spass
      for a town we call new garden and for our unification
      we planted acacias according to a scheme of alternating squares
      the instructions said
      that their roots reach the deepest underground water
      at the waterproof level of clay
      and that at night their flowers
      when the bees put our ancestors' souls to sleep
      swing between the stars
      but our every road still has that look of fermented yellow
      on these three fields
      where white horses black swans hitched in a double carriage
      leap over the time the borderline of one god
      where bees' wings are heavy with ashes
      where every river is of hot milk
      where by the great whirlpool
      wise strangers barter herbs and truth for a bit of cheese
      pulling their wares out of massive locked cloud-boats

and then I find water

I watch the boy atilla on the basketball court
aim a stone at the a half-rotten backboard

and then nothing
when the big rains come again
new grass makes holes through the soles of his sneakers
and gathering itself in a bell-shaped goblet
taunts the big-assed clouds of europe
the great snakelike stormy figures from the asian steppes

and then I find water

down there they say helen sleeps with a star on her forehead
while the watery wind strums the grass grown from her navel
where the carp and the cold birds have made their nest
the fisherman tolya on the other side of the village universe
in short pants full of moldavian fishhooks
dear anatoly rests
rides like a russian apollo in a chariot of stars over a bumpy road
as if shot from a sling evening stars
and the milky way fermented yellow
tolya ran away from the cold earth-star
white daybaba's tongue glued to his back
elijah has no touched the sun
but the grass weeps
but the grass weeps

I'm searching for aphrodite in a town in banat
but I only see rachel's arms in soapsuds up to her elbows
she's afraid of bees
the sun has swollen her mother's eyes
a snake has bitten her
a kigyo apjat
the wasp the snake nailed her father on the cellar door

when she divided the truth beauty grass with the crazy old man
from every haystack breath skims
like when you pour oil into the wind

she died of earth when they pierced her in the knee
now she sleeps in the grass
a phrygian flute gently blowing
the cyprian pollen smells sweet
the wind has uncovered her adamic knee
I dig the plains where someone has already stuck the trident
every second skeleton is pierced with a hawthorn stake
a stake sticks out of the bag of every other man you meet
I dug a city out arad vršac pantčevo starčevo
they say clay is warped by rain
golden masks of a sun now gnawed by green locusts

when I strip the grass from myself the earth remains and images warped by rain

and the locusts
pachytilli migrarii asiatici the storm carried
to this country where even the north wind blows from the east
pyrgomorphellae serbivae with legs like curved sabers
driven by the smoke of nargileh on the trail of arseny's cattle
with the fleece of golden grass
having stopped momentarily on the top of some impassible wall
descended from flat tara to this flat terrain
light lithe dragonflies green locustae viridissimae
from the boeotian fields of teiresias
who sees in the dark and brings she-goats' udders with him
dragonflies sagae serratae mediterranea
on this sea parched like teiresias' breast
on these endless desereted desert fields

beyond the borders of the christian god
like those two brothers among the stars
where a living isan went with a dead isan
on this soil they eat round bread
dragonflies light lithe dragonflies viridissimae
grylli campestres and grylli domestici
swarmed here and caught here
with the music of their grass bows they keep domestic order

which only the mole cricket gryllotalpa vulgaris
poet's countryman and kronos' nephew
constantly breaks through
companion to the snakes
opening small black openings
you might need it yet

when I strip off the shroud the earth still remains and images warped by rain
a mole goes straight through the horse-blanket

an old tribe of midnight priests
left fur hats on our heads
I remember they had no women
through the willows over the river tamish they stole rumanian girls
which I mistook for pike from carpathia
that carry a white pebble under their wing
or a dacian white bone
and lose it in the black mire of the tamish

dry mud green black white

and then that wind
frunza verde lemn uscat

starts blowing through the acacias
somewhere there by the big river
it rounds up the deer
and comes to a stop in the eyes of my xenia

that's why acacia has a flower

MATIJA BEĆKOVIĆ

[1939–]

Bećković was born in Senta and studied Yugoslav litera-
ture at Belgrade University. His first book was the surreal-
ist love poem *Vera Pavladoljka,* published in 1962. Most of
the poems in this anthology come from *Thus Spake Matija*
(1965). Since 1970 and the book *A Man Told Me,* Bećković
has written his poems in a Montenegrin dialect. These poems
are extremely difficult to translate, and yet his very best work
is to be found in these later books of poetry.

If I Knew I'd Bear Myself Proudly

If I knew I'd bear myself proudly
In prison and before judges,
What a trail I'd blaze and endure it all,
Resisting only with my bare hands.

If I knew I'd kick the table
Under my feet and fix the noose myself,
My soul would earn itself eternal life
And my executioner would weep after me.

But I'm afraid I'd start to beg,
To sob, to kneel, to betray everything.
Just to save my bare ass,
I'd spit on all and agree to anything.

Two Worlds

Soon now that day is coming:
We'll send petitions to prison wardens,

Ask them to save us from fear freedom winter
And allow us to serve our time.

So when they finally throw us in chains,
Let the world lose its shameful balance.

Between the two halves that make the world,
May the convicts' half become the bigger one,

And the guards, out of shame and fear,
Some nights plead to stay with us.

No One Will Write Poetry

No one will write poetry anymore,
The immortal themes will abandon the poems
Unhappy with the way they were understood and versified.
Everything that was once the subject of poetry
Will rebel against it and its cowardice.
Objects themselves will express what the poets had no courage to say.
The sea—that ancient subject of poets—will leave poetry forever
And return to its grave where it grew up.
The sun—turned ridiculous,
The starry sky—turned into a cliché,
Will forsake poetry.
The roses will insist on their color
And will not agree to the fickleness of poets.
Word freedom will escape and return to its meaning.
Poets will have no language in which to sing.
Nothing will stand between the poet and poetry,
And so the poems will attack poets
Demanding that they fulfill their promises.
The poets will back away from what they've said,
But everything they imagined and prophesied will catch up with them.
Poetry will demand their lives
So that its metaphors may be true and irrefutable.
In generations to come
No one for any price will want to be a poet.
Future poets will have better ways of spending their time.
The free man will not consent to write poems in order to be a poet—
And yet there's no one other way to be a poet.
A tree—yesterday's poetic symbol—
Will wail from the square of its dark past
And no one will be able to equal its lament

Since it knows itself better than anyone else.
True poets will be against poetry
And all over the world they'll have the same idea:
For the sake of its esteem in the eyes of true poets,
No one will write poetry anymore.

Yevtushenko

September 1968

For days now the ham radio operators wait in vain.
Why are you silent, you who always made so much noise?
If only you were always this quiet,
The way those who are forbidden to speak are quiet.
Where are you now, O great Slavic Soul,
The poet of the emergency room, always on duty?
Are you hibernating or taking a vacation?
Perhaps your heart's mechanism is out of order?
Perhaps you're singing of some even greater injustice?
Perhaps you haven't heard the morning news?
(What will you do when you find out?)
You, at least, didn't spare yourself.
Not a single bullet was fired that didn't make you cry out.
Without tragedy you suffer a writer's block.
They woke you up at midnight to weep over the still-warm corpses.
Your poetry is a calendar of crimes, epidemics, and earthquakes.
To the ends of the earth you traveled to find injustice.
All over the world you sought the reason to love your country.
Your study is the first-class lounge of a jumbo jet.
You stormed out of Siberia to tell us about blacks;
The only surviving glass-tears suicide.
There, where it was permitted to attack—you did.
You forgot where you came from.
The evils you discover, kids learn in the first grade.
You're the only one who made a bundle in a struggle against poverty.
You turned glutton singing of other men's hunger.
Poet made for export, poet of foreign freedoms.
You've become a vending machine of human compassion.
It is enough only to insert in it a slug of sadness
To have tears of ink spill over the page.

Unemployed Orpheus of a country that makes no mistakes.
Humble in Moscow; a lion in Rome.
You condemned the felons sought by Interpol.
You, personally, dug a grave for Steinbeck in Vietnam.
You told off Stalin's moustaches as he lay dead.
They assassinated you before they did Martin Luther King.
His children couldn't get to the casket ahead of you.
You wrote the search warrant for the killer of Bobby Kennedy.
Peddler of other men's defeats and sufferings.
The killers tremble before the judgment of your verses.
The persecution of poets in your homeland
Made you lift your voice against the arrests in Bolivia.
Everybody owes you, except your own people.
The farther the injustice, the louder your voice.
Your moving poems are being read in Prague.
The whole world comes to sob in your handkerchief.
You prove the rule: Who cries a lot, has a long, prosperous life.
Your tear has no native soil.
Russia weeps over a foreign grave.

LJILJANA DJURDJIĆ

[1946–]

Djurdjić studied philology at the University of Belgrade and has three collections of poetry; the first one, *Swedish Gymnastics,* was published in 1977. Djurdjić has done magnificent translations of Sylvia Plath and other American poets.

Unfulfilled Love

I know: My beloved Jonathan Swift
Loved only Stella.

If only I had chosen more carefully
The day and the hour of my birth,

And had it occurred on the Isles,
I would stroll now in her crinoline dress,

With a lovers' seal-ring on my finger,
And with that very special movement

With which she took Swift under the arm,
I'd point to a passerby,

The old glutton and hate-monger.

Lucifer

Lucifer has bad habits
He paints his fingernails green
With Fireproof Polish
On his sideburns
The spittle of last year's garden snails
Waterproof Waterproof
In case the world ends
Only his health counts
Lucifer is my unborn child

Blue Frog Kisses My Sweetheart

An exquisite
Blue frog
Kisses my sweetheart
In the morning she squats on his forehead
At noon she shines in his hair
In the evening she settles next to his heart
My sweetheart is very happy

I Carry My Black Sheep Back to Her Herd

I carry my black sheep back to her herd
So that her sheep-mothers may lick her, suckle her, and make her drink,
And get mud off her, thistle, mildew, and dampness,
The desert sands and soot from her sheep eyes
So she may again stare into the gold greenery,
Into the maternal eyes of her parent sheep

I carry my black sheep back to her herd
So that she may be again white, pure, and infinitely the same,
With a neck ready for ritual slaughter
Over the insatiable earthen vessel
Full of bloody food of the gods

I carry my black sheep back to her herd
So that I can see her head fly,
Her Old Testament head on her bowed sheep-neck,
To hear her generous sheep heart beating
And counting my time, your time, god-knows whose time?
The time of universal slaughter!

RAŠA LIVADA

[1948–2007]

Livada was born in Subotica on the Hungarian border. He studied literature at Belgrade University. His first book, *Spattered with Sweat of the Hands of the Clock,* was published in 1969. He was a much admired and always experimental poet with several fine collections.

Horoscope

You are the imaginary center of the universe eternity that devours
you are not even Yorick or a zero or nothing
you are below zero an iceberg a polar dog an ice cream
of grease and blood and sweat warmed by bear fur
warmed by wheat juices warmed by a dirty joke
inscribed on entrails swollen hearts fetuses:

And the Asiatics, they mow them down like rice fields!

You are neither a positive nor a negative hero a yellow belly
deprived of a voice deprived of wings eggs
beneath a roof you conceal yourself in a supranatural grave
interpreting your sodomite dreams masturbatory dreams
solving crossword puzzles enigmas political conspiracies
you are about 20–25 years old
you practice Esperanto yoga hold your breath
practice shaking hands sending telegrams raising
your eyebrows:

And only you can still clarify the Vedas, Talmud, the Bible, Tao Te Ching, the laws
of Hammurabi, Apocrypha, cromlechs, pregnant goddesses, Bogomils, medieval
hymns, round stones in Guatemala, coral tree, anagoges, Hindu columns!

You despise everything breathing parting your teeth you listen
to the broadcast of the sunrise chase virgins in white socks
chatter about shrinks have an inferiority complex lick deodorized clitorises
commissar of the sexual revolution you have a subscription in your pocket
pace up and down the neighborhood bored from day to day
you beat your head against the gutter watching
the public prosecutors in short pants shopping
while preparing your suicide out of an ambush:

Meanwhile ten million political prisoners divide with mice the worm-eaten
bedboard for lunch!

Like an animal supposedly you bite your wife by the neck and she responds
    in turn
after which you go to a dance and barbecue at the Veterans' Hall
and there meet the ex-professor of geography good evening
you tell her o my god it's you what's your name
and then again o god I traveled much Amsterdam is divine more beautiful
    than ever
those houses without curtains the children so free so young
everything flows o my young friend your clouds are white swans
september is the sweet ache of the passing year
in the woods the deer roars o my god Norway
I'll tell you all afterwards lamb on a spit under a lantern
roasting the sweet ache of the year spur those clouds of yours
in the next world there won't be any hunger dreams and this and that
miraculous uncertainty tell us o god you say:

And only you can still build the pyramids, the cupolas of Kremlin, the stolen
obelisk, Moorish palaces, cathedrals of Köln and Burgos, the giddy villas in
Barcelona, cedar pagodas, pile dwellings, Guggenheim Museum, the Parliament
in the mist, Babylon, Ravenna, Alexandria, Rome!

Afraid of women or simply hating them you are self-centered harsh
which are all signs of effeminacy
you eat pork eat your own innards gnaw slobber suck
with ancestral medals you wipe your ruddy ass
you raise the monument to your meaninglessness
you like clowns and poodles sleep with your teddy bear
from 2 to 4
2 is birth and 4 is death of your week printed ahead

your life you scatter like the pig scatters its trough
you read about the scandals on sports pages pin butterflies by their spine
bend over the coin collection biting your nails
thinking of Maria Theresa stock market in Bern Venetian
gold coins:

And in the land of Basques, Tomás de Torquemada is resurrected!

You catch yourself thinking aloud you wonder how
the stream of consciousness unconsciousness cuts itself off transplants
    of the heart
manners sight customs liver the poetry of the perfect pitch
poetry of ideological idiom
you go to the zoo amazed at the resemblance
you offer pretzels through the bars that keep the animals away from you
you sit in an armchair letting your beard grow
shaving your moustache your underarms hair below your navel
when you happen to have a blade in hand
you simply go crazy abruptly you switch over to the travel ads
you want to distance yourself you cannot:

And the new Spartans play the accordion on the border and wait!

You go to the toilet with a poster of Bermuda Kibbutz Vine Del Mar you flush
the water with an unforgettable scream plunges
lowers itself below the city and farther
through pipes canals through rivers filters and faucets
into your glass of baking soda you eat
the flywheel spins you fall sick fall in love
the flywheel spins the kids grow you don't even notice it
the old men shrink you don't see any of that you say
that's normal and have the impression you're lying

you're given to figures of speech when you're afraid wise courageous
the old petty property owner you vote for the president of the country
hating him with passion in the morning
you are dogmatic in the afternoons skeptical
and always and forever the fan of educational TV

And the Asiatics, during the day they are fighters, at night they are grave diggers,
priests, wailing women!

By all evidence totally deaf you neither respect god nor your own father
you stare at the stars believe in true stars powdered stars
without believing in yourself stars that in turn
do not believe in one another
and thus are cold distant nevertheless you are the life of the party
when you spread out the tarot cards
gargling your mouth with stories about rising prices
and your honor your days yield plenty your nights little
snoring your dreams of sandals torn from the mouth of your madness and
    wisdom
you chose poor man's or rich man's bread you live
in a vast barrel hiding the sun hiding yourself
you are desire under the cover of darkness
in the cycle of collective love you ponder o ascetic
in civilization:

About Bengal, Biafra, Canton, thinking about the origins of bread since bread
is the only tale, the longest tale of what there is never enough of. Philosophy is the
politics of the hungry; politics is the philosophy of the well fed!

Still you listen every night to the classics suddenly impotent
the classics maimed blind crippled full of genius
in the meantime you are kissing a girl

turning the pages of Petrarch and Dante
and other testimonials about the short supply of girls
in the manner of speaking embracing
your own sister and at the same time asking god for forgiveness
and then suddenly there are knocks on your door at daybreak
such are the times
you open there are three of them in raincoats asking for papers
papers have green eyes they tell you
your are pro-Marx pro-Trotsky the stooge of Garodi
you are a Maoist Titoist Castroist
and so in fact are nowhere a mustard seed a quasi-Quaker
a paranoid member of the janitor's grapevine
who listens to the news from badly informed sources
who is nervous because of occasional showers
because of the avalanche in U.S.S.R. because of unregulated native rivers
because of private ownership of weapons and the absence of a target
because of fish oil hair oil machine oil:

And still, only you can explicate the theory of relativity and eventually prove it false; outreason the chronometer from Königsberg; outabsolute the absolute; prove that the superman is a machine. Only you can destroy money, the hammock, the modern state, the four horsemen of the Apocalypse, cultural crises, root beer, the idea of the bullet, cannon, the idea of the sling thrower; only you can prove that labor is in vain, that all sinners will pass through heaven and hell; only you can witness everything and remain blind; only you, with your chopped-lips, still utter tender words!

You in the meantime drinking light beer since dark beer is extinct
since habitually all natives from the shores of Danube
Volga Amazon Yellow River Mississippi drink beer out of cans
squatting on the sidewalk next to groceries bakeries stalls selling flowers
    and pears

beer the smallest common sum of your blood and bones
working with beer through pretzels chips popcorn what about the rain
you ask about the rain I'm undergoing a catharsis
and you have the impression that you've just lied:

And the members of the Atlantic-Warsaw jet-set mix vodka with whiskey,
champagne with gin, which could be bad for one's health, instead of inventing
jealousies, rice bugs, lasers, A-11, X-15, B-52, Mirages, MiG-25's, Telestars,
Cosmos-237's!

And you fight against white-collar crime through newspapermen
men who are the gang-leaders thieves double-spies
spineless killers philistines pushovers sheep who dream of turning into wolves
astonishing if you want to be astonished
your shoes don't fit your eyes
fire water pine-tree earth air everything hurts
oh how trivial you are although always perfected barbered
you collect stamps from Mauritania participate in beauty contests
you get fired in state stores administration bookkeeping
you have exceptionally long fingers you are noticeably older
every day a little less innocent a little less cruel
you are like that because you've been double-crossed
you know some jokes unsuitable for mixed company
your children are dumb you say like your wife who is unfaithful
who takes them for a walk oh how can kids be so stupid
you live in dark ages men on the battlefield
women dance with other women the eternal Ahasueruses croak even the
    Wandering Jew dies
poets read other poets and hate them
poets with a moral at the end of their poems which if you please
has been superseded in these dark times in which you live
your poetry is a dreambook for a concentration camp

no poetry in prosperous times but you just wait
when this dumb Balkan brother of mine drops dead
when they give birth to appetizers roasted suckling pigs your mother and
    my mother
when the celebration of the first and only Serbian defeat is over
there will be born a better brother etc.
you live in terrible times times a calm sea of swamps
after doldrums come even more terrible doldrums
while you still hurry divide your successes into large and small
divide human beings into male and female
among your pals full of pep and invention
though you never talk to yourself never respect anyone:

And still, only you can surpass the Demoiselles d'Avignon, Pietas, Resurrections,
the smile of the Madonna, Broadway Boogie-Woogie, the Parable of the Blind,
triptych of the Garden of Earthly Delights, the three wise kings from the East, the
bull of Altamira, the Green Fiddler, Guernica and Michelangelo, why not!

Of course even then you are unhappy they expect a great deal from you
they curse you you haven't smiled since the last elections
you are sociosurrealist you paint because of fear of death and yet death is the
    greatest freedom
if life was something to cherish so many wouldn't die eh?
you say and then you get excited over ethnic animosity
waiting for the mailman and the outside lefts of the soccer teams
you are somewhere between the electric west and the utopian east
that which was 10 minutes ago utopia is now reality out of reach
you live in wartime everything is collapsing the painter's
line the poet's the mason's brick which is the bomb of the mason
the women's fashion poverty's poverty nothing in the world can undermine
    poverty
you raise the venetian blinds of humanity you ask can stars be profitable

you munch pickles radioactive both you and that pickle radioactive all your
    activity
you claim the stars will pay off you invest in stars
you get on Mars's red on Jupiter's black 13 chips
come on turn them over:

*While an entire metropolis of South Slavs in exile labors for the classic class enemy
of socialism!*

*And an entire Ulster in exile builds a bewildered England shot through with herrings,
tea, and manners!*

However you are an ex-basketball superstar
who angrily claims that the game is not played the way it used to be
and that the future is not what it used to be
now almost old you insist that wisdom comes with age
that everything is like a river everything flows changes
two eyes are better than one man in essence is good
already you weep in her lap about the spilled antifreeze broken transmission
you own a glass for your false teeth a pitcher for your tongue
you are 20 years old you write to the editor of the pornographic weekly
dear editor this is my case tell me can I
and is it enough and will I be able to or not
and you can't:

*And still only you can outplay the consumptive Poles, compose the tenth sym-
phony. Only you can outact Lord Olivier, Orson Welles, Anna Pavlova, Hamlet's
actors. Only you can still outsing the Russian basses deep as their snow, the Italian
butchers—only you, just you!*

*You know Córdoba is distant and lonely, and that it is a fascist Córdoba, and that
it is not lonely!*

*You know that in his end is his beginning, and know that in the doom of the Asian
is the end of Asians!*

*You know that Russia gave thousands millions billions for freedom and took it away
from that many perhaps! For whom was the bride bartered and for what price!*

*You know just about everything under the sun and your worries last less than a
single Bolivian junta!*

And still only you can untie the Gordian knot!

Stop reading this rip it up if you please
you don't need it it's in your blood
make up your mind leave your home full of private
possessions
decide for Christ's sake do something
those bones on Asian slopes used to drink beer
paint sing embrace
decide for the sake of the lost the poor
time spent in waiting's forever lost
stop reading this destroy
this poem
and all other poems
but don't forget them brother!

DUŠKO NOVAKOVIĆ

[1948–]

Author of some dozen collections of poetry, Novaković studied literature in Belgrade and has worked over the years as an editor for some of the leading Serbian literary magazines and newspapers. The poems translated here come from his two recent books: *Scatterbrain's Drawing* (2002) and *The Idiot and His Teacher* (2007).

The Kiosk Was Closed

I went along the avenue farther and farther
And down side streets and even farther than that,
Until I caught sight of you under a light pole,

O, thrown, half-burnt cigarette from a stranger's mouth!
Drawing a breath of your blazing heart
Has meant more to me since that day than any love poem.

Hebraic

I cannot redeem myself

I robbed poorer than myself,
I even hit him, but gently
Only to confuse him.
That was my mistake.

And that I let them catch me
And judge me, and beat me, they who before me
Had skinned him alive,
That was even a greater mistake.

An Avalanche of Questions

Who killed N. N. still needs to be discovered
From the empty shells on the lawn
And the cigarette butts strewn around her
Dried out like dead bumblebees.
Did they smoke together, or did only her killer?
Can the chestnut trees say anything about the crime,
Her final words of disappointment, her last kiss?

Why was N.N. shot like a ragdoll at the fair?
Questions, questions, an avalanche of questions!
Her dirty backpack shows her tastes were modest.
Her simple necklace with a clover leaf
Didn't bring her palaces, golden coaches and luck,
But if she were to come to life now as in a fairy tale,
Everyone would shout, Goddess out of Prakstele's dream!

Regarding the bullet holes in her disfigured head
And the two in-and-out under her left breast,
Will they remain puzzled over for months, then years?
Although on the back of her notebook there's a year's calendar
With some crossed-out days, her monthly periods.
Perhaps the investigation could proceed from these crosses
To the incision on her stomach when she arrives at the morgue,

And continue with the fetus, just beginning to look human
With its inherited maze of cells tied by DNA
To help this disemboweled unknown woman
Not to be just another in a series of unsolved crimes,
Plus a mother of a son she'll never see, who'll never
Smear her lipstick, pull her skirt, suck her teat,
Who'll be his grave within a grave crying for truth.

Pimp

He's that friend who won't let go when he grabs me on the street
As he starts praising his wife, her willingness to yield.
How he knew nothing till he met her, not even to fry an egg sunny-side up.
If only I had a mother and father like this woman he's in love with!

Is it abnormal, doctor, when I lower my eyelids
And I yearn to meet her suddenly and not him on the street,
And plead, since I know how kind she is and I'm not feeling well,
To come quickly to my place, so I may press her naked against me
        for an hour or two like a compress?

Monster

Not even today will the girl her parents are hiding come out.
I see her through the wall as she stares at the wall,
There she is in a dim hallway where shoes are left
Scratching that place covered with hair
Twisting her nose painfully, hating the pointy hot pepper,
Then smearing egg yolk over her face, making herself into a mummy
While keeping her mouth open so that with her screams
She could leave behind the first stage of her ill-defined desire,

Presently she has turned down with disgust two nicely fried cutlets
Thrown the mashed potatoes on the floor like an infant
And in the same wicked way thrown the salad bowl
Over her shoulder, and laughed crazily,
And when the patience of her guardians turned into a gentle reprimand,
She wandered, wandered around her parents with her fork in her hand,
Stabbed her sister in the shoulder and when she saw what she did
Became glum and self-consciously started to tremble,

And soon after being given a valium was put to bed
As if she were being lowered into formaldehyde,
So that untroubled, she sank, without air bubbles
Saved perhaps with Ariadne's ball of yarn in hand,
Or even more lost, even more entangled, mumbling even more horribly
That small unreachable child, all twisted inside,
Could she at least tell me where she has sailed to,
And what island she lives on, so I may swim to her cabin?

Breasts

Bombay, garrulous city, here I am
Already old, on the other side of the world
Remembering your anthill
And the unearthly gaze
Of your Universal Mother,
The warmest I ever saw,
And for that reason wary, making sure
My own eyes are not deceiving me

Since from her left breast she fed
A half-naked, dark-skinned infant,
And from her right a puppy
Hanging by its paws from her neck,
White as the softest cotton ball,
Mother and bitch at the very same time,
And a pump that pumps what the living yearn for,
The joy of her hair spread over them both

So that I ask, as I did then,
What's the point of any poetry, including mine,
If it doesn't strive to grow breasts
She can take everywhere, unbuttoned,
Regardless of being told
"Only primitive, uneducated women" do that
By an official from the ministry ordered
To guide me and explain such things to me.

RADMILA LAZIĆ

[1949–]

Radmila Lazić is one of the best living Serbian poets. She is the author of six collections of poetry, for which she has received several literary prizes. She has published numerous essays on literature and is the editor of an anthology of women's poetry and another of anti-war letters, and the founder and editor of the journal *Profemina*. *A Wake for the Living* was published by Graywolf Press in 2003.

Death Sentences

I was born too late and I am much too old,
My dear Hamlet,
To be your pimply Ophelia,

To let my hair like flattened wheat
Spread over the dark waters
And upset the floating water lilies
With my floating eyes,

To glide fishlike between fishes,
Sink to the bottom like a dead seashell,
Burrow in sand next to shipwrecks of love,
I, the amphora, entangled in seaweeds.

I'd rather you take off my dress,
Let it fall at my feet like aspen leaves
The wind shakes without permission
As if there's nothing to it.

I'd rather have that death sentence:
Eternity of your arms around my neck.

I'll Laugh Everywhere, Weep Wherever I Can

They say I'm easy to fool.
That I buzz like a bumblebee.
That I don't care for work and order.
That I roam around and waste my time.
That I greet dawn at all-night parties.
That I spend my days joyriding.
That I drink gin standing up.
That I scribble poems that way too.
They say I talk too much.
That I beat my gums all day long.
That my tongue flickers like that of a snake.
That it's time for someone to cut it off.
That I could use a punch in the mouth.
That I ought to be pinned like a fly.
They say I must have protection
To go around behaving this way.
They say that I'm a tease.
That I flirt shamelessly with other people's
Lovers and husbands.
That even doing it with a woman is not hateful to me.
Some floozy and some bitch are telling everybody
That I take young boys for a walk
And pluck feathers out of doddering old men.
That I never give any of it for free.
They say that I've gone soft in the head.
That I laugh as if I had a screw loose
If something doesn't please me.
That I sob like a three-year-old child
Wherever I find myself to be.
And I tell them in turn,
I'll laugh everywhere, weep wherever I can.
Life is candied fruit and vinegar,

I add them to my verses in equal amounts.
My syntax is like the tuning of an organ inside the veins.
I burn with a heart 500W strong.
The truth is, I can't warm anyone, but I can burn
With my heart as well as with my tongue.
Which I don't wash or scrub with Brillo.
But whatever I cook up I eat.
Often I was scorched and left unhealed.
Still, I'm no fish on dry land,
Although on dry land I fish for men
With the corner of my eye, the length of my skirt,
Carp fattened with lust
Ready to be caught.
I don't deny it. That's what I do.
I don't give a hoot for all the gossip
Entwined around my name
Like swamp thistle around the reeds.
The sky is above me, that's where I look,
At the stars which I cannot gather.
Nor do I want to.
Let them multiply.
Let them couple and breed.
Let it be like that.

Sorry, My Lord

I'm penniless, my Lord.
Empty heart, empty pussy.
The pockets of my soul are turned inside out.
In my head something tinkles
As in a Red Cross box.
Slip something in my wallet, Lord.

I'm empty and broke.
My heart whistles like a teakettle.
Elsewhere, landscapes burst with beauty.
Here darkness presses on the eyelids.

I squandered everything, blew it away
As if there was no tomorrow.
Now it's Your turn to give me something.
Feed me, heal me
Before You write it down in Your book.
Give me a butt, a lousy nickel.
Give this sinner a cock.

Give me this day.

I neither sow nor reap,
Nor do I weave.
I obeyed Thee, Lord,
Now You take care of me.
I laze in bed past noon,
Loaf around all day with nothing to do.
Nights I spend in bars or over my manuscripts,
Keep vigil, bleed.
In the morning I step on the cold floor of my heart.
Your son, Your darling,

I sniff between his legs
The way a bitch sniffs her litter.
You said: *Do unto others*
As you would have done unto you.
But that man gave me a kick,
Shook me like sand out of a sandal.
I suspect other heels dance now
On his heart's stage
While mine lies hollow like a gutter
Beaten by lethal drops of rain.

Nothing comes easy to me anymore—
Narrow gate, narrow path.
Stop staring at me, Lord.
Gravity won't hold me up.
I'm tipsy, I've lost my footing.
The street grows even more crooked.
My house is even more distant.
Give me Your hand, extend Your finger
Like a torch, not a whip.
Life wails like a mouth organ.
I've thoroughly lost my way.
I can't tell from the birds,
Plants, trees, cardinal points,
Sweetwater fish from the deep-sea kind,
The source from the mouth of a river,
The dreams over which I wade
From the street where I swing my hips.

Many times I fell in love forever.
My heart was a hot stove.
Now the jug is broken.

Let there be sex unstained by love
Is my slogan now.

Every other desire I shook off
Like raindrops from a coat.
Have mercy, Lord.
I sing of a drowned soul
Which I can't drag to the shore.
My hands hang like wild game.
Help me! Rescue me!
Give me—mouth-to-mouth!

I love strong drink, violent men,
And other such foolish things.
I confess to You, Lord,
Not a single sin eluded me.
Like Your own body
My heart is a pincushion.

Sorry, Lord.
I'm neither Martha nor Magdalena.
I'm what You spat out, Your discharge.
Now weigh it all on Your scales.
Don't tip them, don't cheat on me.
Go and weigh them.
Blind my heart, take away my sight
To suffer and pay.
Lord, have mercy on me.

Anthropomorphic Wardrobe

There's no more room. We are full.
Everything we stored, layer by layer,
Folded, packed in as if bandaging wounds.
Belongings we hung by a hook,
Belongings we lined up on hangers,
Winter wishes, summer dreams,
Sunsets, snowy peaks,
What's yours-what's mine, sighs and sobs—
Now shifted every which way.

Forgotten. Taken down in a hurry.
Thrown in the corner. Turned inside out.
What is indispensable and what is less so
Thrown on top of one another.
Once made to measure, then grown short,
Grown too tight, faded or shiny—it's all here.

Adam's little broken rib.
The plucked angel's wing.
Venus's fur and love-stain.
Rings. Combs. Ghosts. Moths.
No one can find anything here.
Where is it? Turn it upside down! Rummage!
Lost, then found again.
Rejected, then cherished again.
Cobwebs sway. The mouse gnaws.
The butterfly spreads its wings.

Torn in the eye. The sea on its last breath.
Night-day. Loves-doesn't love.
Throw it, keep it. Give-take.
This to the dry cleaners. This to the devil.

This to the Salvation Army. And this—not in your life!
The creases of lust. Washed-out heart.
Weepy muslin. Ariadne's thread.
Adjectival lace. Aorist.
Sentence-rags. Flake of words. Peek out
Of drawers, dangle. Expired. Eternal.
Trickle. Ooze. Shed tears. Drip pleasures.
The snivel of time passing. Used-up life.

Evergreen

I've had enough of lonely women.
Sad. Miserable. Abandoned women
Whose souls float like bottles
Thrown in the sea with a message.
Enough of professional mourners.
Enough of companions, sisters, dispensers of condolences.
Old maids and marrying types,
Eternal widows whose hearts leak and drip
Like rusty faucets.
Enough of that funeral march.
I don't want anything more to do with you.

Enough of Mother Hubbards
And faithful wives with their eyes lowered—
The guardians of last year's snows and Gardens of Eden.
Enough of your herbariums and picture albums,
Dried up beavers and ironed-out wrinkles.

Enough of your frozen talents
Simmering with His favorite dish in a pot.
Your black liver and fried brains.
Your empty beds and waxed floors
Over which moonlight slides
Instead of Shakespeare's beast with two backs.
I have nothing in common with you.

Enough of your big asses,
Double chins, circles under the eyes, abortions,
Diets, depilations, hairdos,
Low-cut dresses, high heels.
Enough of playing footsie under the table,
The meaningful look under the eye,

Auctions and bargain sales:
Who-will-do-what-to-whom.

Enough of your aperitifs and desserts.
Young studs and sugar daddies.
Your sweet poisons,
Loved to death till death do us part,
Your Seventh Heaven that rests
On the tip of His shoes.
Your Holy Mangers in the crotch of His legs.
Enough of your: "Our listeners request."
Your "nevermore" is an old song,
Evergreen of your late springs.
You'd give anything for a man
In the image of a helpless god,
Adam's rib.
I don't want anything more to do with you.

I'd like to be dancing on a trapeze,
Walking on high wire, taming lions.
Through a fiery hoop I'd jump
Into everyone's throat or heart,
So I can be born again in labor pains.
I'd do everything the same way and everything differently
With his beloved head on my belly—
As on Salome's plate.

I'll Be a Wicked Old Woman

I'll be a wicked old woman
Thin as a rail,
The way I am now.
Not one of those big-assed ones
With buttocks churning behind them,
As Celine said.
Not one of the good-natured grandmas and aunties
Against whose soft and plump arms
It is nice to lay one's cheek.
I'm more like a scarecrow
In our gardens full of rosy tomatoes
Like children's cheeks.
There are some old crones
Who are both vivacious and angry as a bee
With eyes on top of their heads
Who see everything, hear everything and have an opinion—
Grumblers since birth.
I'll squawk and chatter all day,
Cackle like a hen over her chicks
About the days when I was
A young, good-looking girl,
When I led boys by the nose.
Colts and stallions I tamed
With the flash of an eye, the flash of my skirt.
Passing over infidelities and miseries
The way a general passes over his lost battles.
I'll be free to do anything as an old woman,
Among things I still can and want to do
Like playing bridge or dancing
The light-footed dances of my days.
I'll spin and trip on my sticklike legs,
Attached to my body like toothpicks to a kabob.

That old hag can sure boogie!
The young smarties gathered around me
Will shout and applaud.
An old woman like a well-baked bun with sesame seeds,
That's what I'm going to be like.
I'll stick between everyone's teeth, as I did before,
While with a wide hat and dresses down to the ground
I stroll through landscapes of my past life.
Smelling the furze, admiring the heather,
On every thistle catching my undergarment—my soul.

NOVICA TADIĆ

[1949–]

Novica Tadić was born in 1949 in a small town in Montenegro. He has published fourteen books of poetry. He is the recipient of all the major Yugoslav and Serbian literary prizes. His work has been translated into many languages. A book of his selected early poems, *Night Mail,* was published by Oberlin University Press in 1992. In 2009, *Dark Things* was published by BOA Editions, and *Assembly* was published by Host Publications.

Toys, Dream

Tonight my mother was born

her infant cry
filled our house
at the outskirts

bathed and so clean
I wrapped her
                in a diaper
and laid her in a crib

from the corner I brought
toys
      blew twice
into a small plastic trumpet

Made the black wooden horse rock

A Feather Plucked from the Tail of the Fiery Hen

Let them rest peacefully in ice.
I'm never coming back
to my native mountains,
trees, mists.
I don't give a damn about
forest clearings, mushrooms, wise weasels,
ditches full of last year's snow.

I don't care about wild pigeons.

I'm the Fiery Hen,
I sing at mid-day
lost in the crowd on the square.

My long pole is my home.

Lord, I'm so glad
to be so rich,
to be so ridiculous.

I see everything with my round eyes.

Oh I'm both dread and happy disposition,
conflagration over all things.
Under my fire-wing
lies the mad world.

I'm the fire that gives the Egg its shape.
I'm the fire that shapes.
I'm fire.

I'm the fiery scold.
The first monster.
The queen of terror
on whose every feather
burns one living
monstrous image.
I'm the monstrous image.
Queen of dread.
Fear at mid-day,
scream,
panic and flutter.
Cramp and light.
Between tearing sounds
the one tearing sound.
The deaf and mute sign
on the frightened mouth.
Golden talon,
golden will,
golden beak.
A beak
that nightly
drinks the slumbering
brains.
Feathers, bones,
and blood that
flies.

Song to the Lamb

Lamb indestructible lamb
You who loaded with crystals crossed the mountain
Lamb from the most distant cave
Lamb who peed on the black stones
Yo-yo turning on the highest rock
Lamb with fleece of bones
                    In the deepest night
You who bleat among the oldest trees
                    Lamb who remembers
Lamb grazing and browsing the human brain
Lamb who imagined the blue sky
Lamb of all the firmaments
Lamb who leaves behind wild strawberries
Lamb who makes the open eyes open again
Lamb with deepest waters
                    In your burning eyes
Lamb indestructible lamb

Lamb of dark forest
With a wreath of needles in your fleece
                    Lamb of juniper bush
With a purple berry in your hoof
Lamb of the deepest abyss you descend down the mountain
Lamb spreading the scent of fir trees at night
Lamb with snowballs of last year snow on your back
Lamb with white teeth O long-legged Lamb
Who will kill me

Terrifying lamb
You dug for me tonight an appropriate grave
                        In the midst of the world
Where you'll settle down finally settle down
The way your tongue settles down between my jaws
                        Accurately settles down

Antipsalm

Disfigure me, Lord. Take pity on me.
Cover me with bumps. Reward me with boils.
In the fount of tears open a spring of pus mixed with blood.
Twist my mouth upside down. Give me a hump. Make me crooked.
Let moles burrow through my flesh. Let blood
circle my body. Let it be thus.
May all that breathes steal breath from me,
all that drinks quench its thirst in my cup.
Turn all vermin upon me.
Let my enemies gather around me
and rejoice, honoring You.

Disfigure me, Lord. Take pity on me.
Tie every guilt around my ankles.
Make me deaf with noise and delirium. Uphold me
above every tragedy.
Overpower me with dread and insomnia. Tear me up.
Open the seven seals, let out the seven beasts.
Let each one graze my monstrous brain.
Set upon me every evil, every suffering,
every misery. Every time you threaten,
point your finger at me. Thus, thus, my Lord.
Let my enemies gather around me
and rejoice, honoring You.

I Ask

is the
dinner
ready

I ask
someone who
behind my back
in the nonexistent room

rearranges
the plates

Jesus

Jesus
Our Jesus
Our Jesus a pincushion

Thief

Drags his tail on the ground, damn thief
Feeds his thousand mice
Eats, drinks up, guzzles
All day long sings the blues
Parties like no one
Shears with happy ears
Drags everything down down
Trades truly with hollow gold coins
Steals and filches
Leaves in testament walls, ashes, air
Stuffs his gravelike sack

Crawls into the egg of a snake

Runs backwards toward chaos

Nobody

He shows me tonight
his hair of wire glass and flowers
doubled-edged lips
five-pointed tongue

Ah he unbuttons
his silk vest—
he has a body after all—
a gold watch

And in the meantime meantime
in the shadow of his trousers
instead of feet
he has two little wheels
devilish little wheels

I Run with a Pair of Compasses Stuck in the Back of My Head

Down below
I run from street to street
down below
from street to street O Lord
with a pair of compasses
stuck
in the back of my head

The Rose

In a glove shop
I bought
          black gloves
on a stone ax
          I sharpened my awl

So come to me this evening
knock on my window

Through my window this evening
throw me a rose

The Fool

The one disappearing
behind the corner
one-eyed
and hunched over
with razor-tongue
the lout
who slits
the throats of rabbits
carries through the city
the bowl
to gather the blood in
and a sharp ax
under his arm

Everywhere spreading
the smell of snow

Pocket Watch

Under it a puddle of blood
So it looks like
It's doing its work
Making someone inside march

When the cuckoo bird flies in
It goes quiet
           doesn't dare make a peep
Covers itself with metals ears
          and leaves me
          to her motionless
          supervision

Text, Silk

You closed your eyes, crossed your hands
In the deepest household darkness
over a text full of heresies.

You, too, take up the devil's business,
you, too, be the evangel of love.
Into our body's every opening, grace descends.

The old, already forgotten crime,
will give you a giant's strength.
Place your hand on the holy thigh at night.

That's the only way the silklike
Holy Ghost comes down from heaven
among the cursed.

At the Hairdresser

(phantasmagoria)

At night at the hairdresser's
The angel with bright scissors
And a monstrous comb draws near
To the archangel's funnel-like ear:

If God is dead, if he truly fell in
The abyss, let's place instantly
On his empty throne, the hairdresser
Who does our hair so well.

The Night Game of the Maker of Faces

From his mouth he takes out
Two petrified butterflies
Ties them with black thread and pulls them
Behind him
              between the moved
Furniture
             the walls look at each other
The ceiling is surprised
                  the butterflies
Hop
And land on each other
              so that his smile
Falls among things
So that he goes on smiling behind his back

Little Picture Catalogue

1
In a ghost town
dogs roam
among dead dogs

2
in a blind alley
a boy wheels the halo
of the holy mother

3
in someone's backyard
a crucified
hen

4
from the pipe of a customer
in a whorehouse
a woman's black stocking
rises like smoke

5
in the anteroom
many shoes overcoats
hats gloves
but the house empty
not one human face
        to be seen

6
unknown massive gray
objects above the waters
of salvation

Die

I threw
A single die
On the table
Of black marble

Saw
Not one side
Of the cube
Had a mark or a number
There was
Nothing

Dark Things

Dark things open my eyes,
raise my hand, knot my fingers.

They are close and far away,
in a safe hideaway
beyond nine hills.

Night is their kingdom,
and this day, just breaking,
is their cloak of light.

No force can revoke them,
untangle them, explain them.

They stay where they are,
in our breasts,
stirring in our hearts.

Magpie the Witness

What you took out
on a newspaper
to throw out in front of the house,
you showed to a magpie
who flew away

full of greed and malice

to spread the news about your crime
of which you know nothing
before royal thrones
and humpbacked judges
and to testify against you finally.

In a Train Station, Dream

Small, bent over, gray,
I'm sitting with arms crossed
on my luggage.

I ask nothing of no one.
Wait for no one.

I don't know where I've come from
nor where I'm going.

In the trunk are my books,
In the suitcase my shirts.

I packed everything I had.

On my head I wear
a cap of many colors,
my great pride and joy.

MILAN DJORDJEVIĆ

[1954–]

Born in Belgrade, Djordjević is a short-story writer and essayist and a translator as well as a poet. His first book of poems, *On Both Sides of the Skin,* came out in 1979. Since then, there have been seven more, the latest of which has just been published. He has received most of the prestigious literary awards in Serbia for his collections of poetry and his stories and essays and has had his work translated into German, Polish, Romanian, Hungarian, Slovak, Portuguese, Macedonian, and now English.

Overcoat

Overcoat lies. On the floor.
Without a drop of blood in it.
Overcoat lies. Weary.
Crumpled, discarded and black.
—Overcoat! Overcoat! Overcoat!
—Dear brother! Rise! Rise!
At least kneel next to your
Milan Djordjević!
Dear brother, guardian of my solitude,
beaten with rain, snow,
curses, flatteries.
Rise! Rise!
I will feel your empty pockets
with my hands.
They'll flutter their wings in them.
Inside your gaping sleeves
I'll let the care-worn little animals
that are my arms crawl!
So it may begin to breathe
and open its eyes, shudder,
then move one sleeve,
spread its wings, fly, caw
and drape me with its darkness.
I, who am its blood and guts.

Spud

In a deep tomb he lay,
a dark-hued pharaoh resting in peace.

In private, he shed grief-stricken tears
for the honest mud where he was hatched.

Here he is now on a plate, arrogant, boiled,
crowned with parsley, smeared with butter,

solitary like a newborn, he who saved
from hunger both the damned and the just.

Look, a thin knife cuts him in half.
Look, a fork sticks out of his back.

But, friend, don't be sorry for them.
Don't look darkly on the world of potatoes,

since other saviors in sacks are sprouting
hoping to see the polestar some clear day.

Silence and Snow

The snow falls on the frozen earth. The snow falls.
In the silence I think I hear the sound of its fall,
like the rustle of a cloth or the crackling of a fire.

In the silence as thick as billions of particles
of an exploding Niagara,
or the slide of some Himalayan avalanche.

In a photograph from Japan, swarming with snow
there are monks in orange robes
under umbrellas made of bamboo.

They were caught walking past a garden wall
and some black pine trees arrested forever
in the silence solidified by the falling snow.

This silence is eternal and never to be repeated.
She's the gentleness and softness of bird feathers,
the bliss of an October afternoon the color of honey.

She's the dust from wooden bookshelves,
the yearning of an old man for the carelessness
and the endless sweetness of childhood, Paradise,
as fresh as the taste of just-picked strawberries.

The Rain Wants to Kill Itself

With its fingers the rain stains your window and mumbles.
It wants to come in and kill itself.
I see you are in bed and couldn't care less.
In the dark. Naked. Couldn't care less.
Your hair loose. Your thighs spread open.
And there, in plain sight, black moss.
Your left middle finger busy, busy!
Villain, searching for the red crest.
While golden honey already oozes.
You call me from your delirium tremens.
Me already changed into a crow.
I fly down into your lap and peck, peck.
And then in my beak carry the caught fish away,
to go play cards and drink.
While the rain with its fingers
makes stains over your windowpanes and mumbles,
counts its beads,
wants to come in and kill itself.

Love Poem

My dear Nothing,
with love and words
I keep trying
to breathe life into you.
With so much flirting
I'm becoming a part of you.

My dreamy Nothing,
daughter of human nothingness,
I want you dead and gone,
but you are indestructible,
truly untouchable
like everything imagined.

Will I be free of you,
one day perhaps?
Or will I hide you deep within me
while all around me you give birth
to monsters and specters?

You'll whisper the same stories,
pour over me
the same black ashes
and desert rains
without erasing the bloodstains
of my childhood.

My sweet and formless,
bloodless and colorless,
best-loved Nothing,
with what eyes shall I look at you
to see you truly
and remember your face forever?

A Man in a State of Rebellion

tonight someone will fuck someone else
while statesmen negotiate
untie the knots on neckties long underwear
and tense international situations
while secretly they scratch their balls under the table
tonight someone will jump from the tenth floor
leaving in the washer dish rags and dirty dishes
someone will throw himself from a moving train
forgetting to shut the window and door behind him
there'll be a draft aborting hundreds of dead insects
someone will cry next to the open refrigerator
watching the stars while gnawing a pork rib
the summer cactus will flower tonight in the garden
and I will grow nauseous of that small manifestation of life
huddled like a carnivorous worm on the bottom of a glass
I'll tip over the glass and the piss pot
stuff my mouth ears nose and eyes with cotton
and shout stubbornly into the molehill of my flesh
so the deaf hear me so that their heads turn into a bell and a clapper
I'll make all my bones rattle with my voice
I'll protest against I don't-even-know-what
against gravity and newly printed useful lies
against everything in the perfectly ordered deodorized world which doesn't exist
I who do not exist in a country that doesn't exist
and thus with my nonexistent cold weapons
I will tenderly kill the dog the cat the canary and wife
lower the window curtains break the light bulbs
set the furniture on fire let the boiler
explode while I pour foam out of a bottle of shampoo
chase the mosquitoes and flies break the wall with a hammer
telephone the president and in a humble voice
wish him much success in his career

and follow that with shouts of idiot and a promise
that I'll treat him to a drink spiked with poison
then I'll rip up the electric cord and cut my veins
convinced that from now on everything will go well
I'll take my clothes off wish myself goodnight and lie down calmly
daydreaming in bed like a nearsighted god
with the TV always at the touch of a finger
its cyclops's bloody eye staring down at him benevolently

NINA ZIVANČEVIĆ

[1957–]

Zivančević was born in Belgrade. She is a literary critic, journalist, and translator as well as a poet. She lived for several years in New York, where she wrote in English, and now resides in Paris. New Rivers Press published a book of her poems, *More or Less Urgent,* in 1980. The poems in this anthology come from her books *The Spirit of Renaissance* (1989) and *At the End of the Century* (2006).

Florence

I rise early with a slight nausea.
I rise early with the old green Ghibelline hat . . .
hurry into the city of deadly poisons,
I leave behind me the city of lagoons wonder-working glass
of the Venetian Christmas beads and stroll
through the excrement of dogs, always through that excrement
the feeling "sarebbe, devi essere mio" in our wake,
dark city with the emblem of the lily
dark city with the apothecary shop where Dante's house used to stand,
I hurry through the street of the compassionate Giotto
through the mud where that woman
was afraid of walls and insisted that they had ears,
I walk through dark houses with private graves,
I walk through the city of fears,
I hurry through the city of poisons with my ridiculous green hat
I play with the marble lily there where words should play
drowned in the Arno of all fears, since truly
whoever once enters this place never again will find the way out,
while I walk on the cobble where flea markets
become fleas climbing the Renaissance trees,
and there on the wall of yellow mortar—who might be hiding there?
Behind all that mud, mortar, and chocolate—who is left to dream?
While I walk through the capital of the lily and thin leather,
while I walk through the poisonous streets
of lilies, pink linen, soccer, and witty banter,
the city of medieval streets . . .

Duende

He, who has so much duende—like me—
takes me at night into his dark chamber
when owls hoot I feel a strange and fearful
craving that falls all over the room
like red silk
that brocade of desire
this midnight made of fingers
this unbearable desire to touch
the piano keys
the membranes of the organ
sounding like a waterfall
that wrecks itself and beats on the walls
of the labyrinth in which we stroll
and at times speak in a whisper
more tender than the eyes that
also meet in the appointed corner
where I see how happy are those
who carry duende within them,
because truly I'm happy since he . . .
he too is happy with him . . .

Kindergarten Curse

I tell him, don't be mad at me,
you small and eccentric creature,
give me back my rags and mediterranean moonlight
and my vasko popa,
we are so tired of this game
in which silk means nothing anymore
and I'm again afraid of sharks
while I dream again with you,
our bed has turned into something
I wouldn't even tell my best girlfriend about,
things are so bad, still
we could, or you could, exchange your marbles
for my plastic super girl, we could
ride in flying saucers
until my soul darkens so much
and I trip and hurt my knee,
we ran and played hide-and-seek
during our honeymoon—much too slowly,
so I ask of you, give me back my worn-out gods
and my enameled idols,
the blue landscape we loved
has vanished, in my picture book
I find only something sad and horrible,
I'm speaking to you, do you hear,
—I'm asking you nicely . . .

A Poem with a Tilde in the Title

I'm sad and serious
like the little Donna Infanta imprisoned
in Velázquez's painting, while I watch
my silly royal retinue with remote
and soulful eyes, bending over a ray of light,
directed at young princes,
niños, and dueñas, and while I shrug
the pearls of dust off my lonely shoulders,
and hide in my curls their friendly deceits,
and wait for my dwarfs and polite servants
to bring me the indifferent cup of chocolate . . .

I'm sad and serious as if yesterday
I sent a fleet of explorers
to search for a new continent and bring me back fresh spices,
golden idols, new refinements,
and the exaggerated insults of distant monarchs,
soft fabrics and unusual toys in the shape
of the bleeding human heart, while knowing
that all they will bring me back
are barbaric seashells, effigies of gods
with the hollow, painted mouths
who are trying to say something simple and terrifying
that is like a whisper, a bottomless howl . . .

Ode to Western Wind

O, great great Western wind,
lift me up and take me back
to people and places I loved,
save me from this neoclassical order
and its stupidities,
take me as far as you can from Gard du Nord
from which they took
200,000 Jews to camps,
so that not a single one came back,
carry me away from Europe
poisoned with wars and plagues,
as far as possible from the United States
where people die in hunger and ignorance,
take me back to Serinda where to breathe is more important
than sublime thought and moving about,
take me to the make-believe land of poetry
and keen spirit
where women don't speak of equality
and where men dance the tango all day
and all night,
lift me high, wind
and make me forget
this terrible ever-present reality,
since, if the spring has indeed come
why am I trotting
so far behind it?

Letter to Tsvetaeva

Ah, now our time has come, Marina.
You visit me at night while I sit alone
with a glass of wine in hand
—you who do not need a key—
for you the most secret door of my room
is always open:
abandoned by our mothers,
we both loved children and poetry,
and hated Paris and poverty,
wearing the one and only dirty dress,
we kept clear of landlords and cops.
We both had blue eyes, many lovers,
and the incapacity to live with anyone.
Ah, I almost forgot: our fathers, too,
had similar jobs—they occupied themselves
with museums and art . . .
Still, I got angry yesterday
when someone called me Marina . . .
I'm neither important nor odd enough
to send daily reports to Beria . . .
How furious I was that you hanged yourself!
What courage, what a double cross, what a lie,
what a betrayal of poetry . . .
Marina, I'm a child as you can see,
about you and life I really know nothing.

DANICA VUKIĆEVIĆ

[1959–]

Vukićević lives in Belgrade where she works as a high school teacher. She has four collections of poetry, the latest of which is *Bow and Arrow* (2006), from which these poems come from.

Ave

It's dangerous to live
Smell the enemy
And play up to your lover
It's dangerous to sit
On the beach and listen
To the sun loafing
It's dangerous to stroll
Touch brooding tree trunks
Shake hands in the park
And swing
It's dangerous to live
Sit on the couch
And read a book
Dangerous to think and laugh
Dangerous to yearn
And take a bath
Dangerous to look at things
Dangerous to sleep
And say no in a dream
Dangerous to be good looking
And have oneself photographed
As if death didn't exist

Rocking

Tree tops hung
Like flowers out of the sky
The sky had a pleasant glow
Even though the night was letting down
Its fish hook
We flew
One could hear us bumping
With our bodies (whoosh)
Into the sphere
Heading toward the tiny
Broken up moon.

Novica Zdravković Was Here

O, my cowboy
Huge cockroaches
Are going by
My hands smell
Of the hospital and the pharmacy
That cannot be
Forgotten
On the road to exotic-domestic,
Dust, pure, golden
The drunken old man works like a slave
One more season . . .
The heat hums making me sleepy
Watermelons, tomatoes,
By the side of the road
Heaviness came from above, from inside
The inebriated blood dries out
The sun, the sun, doctor
The constant brightness: of the road, the water,
The leaves
Around the monastery a plenitude of forces
Locked in, the clouds pass
I don't need to look, don't need
To see
Houses smell of humidity
Wine flies fall in the eyes
Before the storm that is still to come . . .

O, I peeked out of
The window.
Opened it.
Cold. Freezing. Calm. Wind.
Entered. And stayed.
I was remembering. Immoderately.

I throw food to the yellow dog.
Pigeons. Coal miners. Lions.
You can't imagine all the things that are here.
Industry.

False weariness, neglect.
Waiting. Voices.
White light. Long night.
The wheels of trains and cars pass by.
I hear them . . .
The motor turning over in bitter cold.
Someone will come.
Lie down. Sleep. With me.
We'll be warm.
Warm . . .

Twilight
You're my village
A wheat field with crows
A field
I sing walking
Through the twilight
Hold on to the hem of my skirt
Cut the gold
Get up before dawn
Barely lie down before
The first crack
Thin fingernail the moon slides off
Pumpkins grow
The tree tops begin to toll

At the edge of the bed
I sat
In the dead of the night
The clock was ticking
O, clock. The hours
Ticked away
My head was spinning
From so much travel.
Poppies dressed in yellow
In red
Waiting for someone to call,
To pass over in silence,
To announce the news.
The rosy color vanished
From things.
The garden grew smaller
Darkness rose over all,
Regally, like
Pain.
And hissing, I remembered you
Father
(not knowing how to cry
or to be happy)
Staring dumbly
In the madhouse
At the very ceiling
Others were staring at . . .
O, father.

DRAGAN JOVANOVIĆ DANILOV

[1960–]

The most prolific and widely translated poet of his genera-
tion, Danilov is not only a poet, but also a novelist, essay-
ist, and an art critic. He studied the history of art and now
works in a museum in the town of Užice. The poems here
come from his collection *The House of Bach's Music* (1993),
Concert for No One (2001), and *Homer of the Outskirts*
(2003).

Room Carried on Wings

I, too, had my travels.
Last night I read in the armchair in the corner,
and today I'm under the spider web
on the other side of the room—a cat asleep in my lap
since she knows there's no reason to get involved.

Speaking of solitude, I distance myself from it.
I'm not reexamining the frontiers of the void
nor the possibilities of the poetic language;
I've no interest in the shrill intricacies of the epic,
the feats of Kazakh chieftain; I don't have
my own website on the internet; my wild shadow
is alone in a room gone wild and terrifying.

Tender like a foot sole of a child, I left myself
in some seaside town for the night
to descend and cover my body with the immensity
of someone who is calm and who is everywhere.

Motherland, I'm your poor child,
I'm a piece of paper on which a heart beats.
The smell of the sea dreamed of long ago
wafts into my chaos, it watches me with eyes of a blind man,
tells me that I'm the great traveler
who doesn't budge from his home.

There, too, I had my travels.

Cursed City

City
cursed city
wrapped in fog
in which faded images flit
charred city of frayed conscience
sad rag of the world
ugly city like an iron cage
I once thought was beautiful
like the gait of a pregnant woman

Vomited city
hometown pious woman
cursed like the year
covered with wounds and rips
not even your unexpected gentleness
will visit me in the hospice
where I spent my whole life

Cursed cursed city
from whose claws I'll never tear
the empty vessel of my body
city of ghosts
where again I seek my refuge

Here I'm made of ice suffocating
the day is dying and there's no one to lengthen it
despite the rumor about me
I'm inside a cauldron-like voice
of someone who doesn't exist
I have no other body no other city
nameless
my hand only clings on to the fire

Two Continents of Skin

In the pupil of the eye of this day
it's as quiet as in a pharmacy.

Leisurely like a scent
you spoke as if through a veil
with you in bed
it was like being with a cat
but much much softer.

The obvious too is a fiction—
all we have are these fingers
and two continents of skin.

Hidden from evil eyes,
gently we shivered
like a starry sky over a village.

The soul and the book are immeasurable.
Our most beautiful words
we said with the palms of our hands.

There's never been a world
except the one that still has to be created.

Confiding to a Shadow

I don't see what I see; here the city ends
between buildings that are an elbow's length
from one another, a crane reconnoiters
as if it knows the essence of the problem.

Middle-aged woman passes in the street in her dark
illegibility, a boy and a girl, exceedingly young,
are walking on the narrow path that leads into the woods.

On one of the balconies, a sparrow, like a stiff cut-out
of a pre-war corporal, pecks at crumbs of some untruth
about the world; a child plays with another bird; something
glows within him, while down below the top of a chestnut
tree is so beautiful, I am frightened.

That fear that grows deep inside no one sees,
though it exists fiercely like the monument to Prince Michael
on the Square of the Republic in the hot,
flickering light of the afternoon
when reason consents to be deceived.

There's a war on and it's dreary
like those easy-to-digest and shallow books
of briefly famous authors
who play with subcultural phenomena.

A cat stretches by the trash can, clearly
keeping mum about some deep matter,
she watches me as if for a moment
I've grown dear to her, and her eyes, blue like the limo
in which they shot Kennedy, are possibly
the last thing this day has to offer.

The Key

I lost the key that just a moment ago
was in the palm of my hand.

The first-person pronoun at all times, as a rule,
knows too much, though it's not always like that.

There, I lost my key,
I misplaced it somewhere,
or a strange hand stole it,
threw it in the war,
cemented it perhaps in the foundation of a building.

I don't know where my house key is,
and the world exists for me only in my house
where my solitude nourishes itself
with the bread of my solitude.

Suspicions make a nest wherever they can,
to observe from there the unfolding events.

On some wild beach where the fingers
of lovers intertwine and build a labyrinth,
there, perhaps, is my key.

In this world, it's worth living only
for things of which one can speak in a whisper.
The rest is not worth mentioning.

VOJISLAV KARANOVIĆ

[1961–]

Born in Subotica, Karanović has lived in Novi Sad where he
has worked as drama editor on the local radio and as poetry
editor of a prestigious literary journal, *Letopis Matice Srpske.*
He has published six books of poetry and has translated
English literature.

Garden

In the garden in which the planet earth
sways on a branch, all's quiet.
No one makes a move.

With strong gusts, time bends
the top of a tree, but the fruit
dithers, it's still hangs there,

so high, no one
can reach it.
No one can pick it.

The petal from which it hangs
is as thin as a thought. When it breaks,
the fruit falls and rolls on the ground,

but *that* only the dead can see.
In their gaze, it rolls,
in their dream, it stops.

In the Forest

The earth has goose bumps, don't you think?
Whence these trees, this growth
of tangled grasses, thunderbolts,
rotten leaves, broken
twigs.

A caterpillar crawls
over a green leaf
moving slowly like your days,

it nears the edge
that divides the leaf from the air
always a bit cold and unreal.

Like letters of an
incomprehensible language,
the ants swarm on the ground.

You get goose bumps when the air
touches you with its invisible fingers.
Whence these tangled words, the forest
of sentences, the quiet clearings.

Choice

It could've been different.
I could've been a tree. A maple,
For example.

I could've been a reed
Whooshing to itself.

Or a wild duck
Vanishing
In the shrubbery.

I may not have been asking
As the day breaks, why is the Danube
Shivering under the blanket of morning.

No, choice is like
A trained bird dog
Who has smelled my blood.

I've become a living cage
Trailing a feathery orb
Behind me.

I Saw

Under a plane tree that glistens
in the splendor of April sunlight,
in a puddle left
in some hollow in the asphalt,
in whirling dust,
in footprints, in ashes
shaken from a cigarette,

in the beating of a heart
sharp as the teeth of a saw,
in the cut tree trunks,
in the fumes that hover
over the road, the fire that turns over
a page of crumpled paper,

in the fingers that thumb newspapers,
in the picture in the obituary,

I saw, I'm sure,
that shadow that slides, grows distant,
and the light charging
as it shines on, illuminates everything in its way,
everything inside itself.

CHARLES SIMIC is a poet, essayist, and translator. He was born in Yugoslavia in 1938 and immigrated to the United States in 1954. Since 1967, he has published more than twenty books of his own poetry, as well as books of essays, memoirs, and translations. Simic has received the Pulitzer Prize in Poetry, the International Griffin Prize, a MacArthur Fellowship, and the Wallace Stevens Award. He recently served as United States Poet Laureate. He is Emeritus Professor of the University of New Hampshire, where he has taught since 1973.

This book was designed by Rachel Holscher. It is set in Arno Pro type by BookMobile Design and Publishing Services, and manufactured by Versa Press on acid-free paper.